C000214745

She's Just... Alice

She's Just... Alice

Joanna Whittaker

Every effort has been made to contact those whose permissions we have needed to print this book. We are very grateful for the books and songs that have been quoted here and hope we have done you warm justice.

Matador
9 Priory Business Park,
Wistow Road, Kibworth Beauchamp,
Leicestershire. LE8 0RX
Tel: 0116 279 2299
Email: books@troubador.co.uk
Web: www.troubador.co.uk/matador
Twitter: @matadorbooks

ISBN 978 1838593 896

British Library Cataloguing in Publication Data.
A catalogue record for this book is available from the British Library.

Printed and bound by CPI Group (UK) Ltd, Croydon, CR0 4YY
Typeset in 11pt Adobe Caslon Pro by Troubador Publishing Ltd, Leicester, UK

Matador is an imprint of Troubador Publishing Ltd

This book is dedicated to my loving husband,
David, and our wonderful sons, Ben and Matthew.

All proceeds that come from the sale of this book are going to a charity called Rosy, based in Oxford. They provide nursing care for sick youngsters and fund additional respite nursing care at home for children with chronic, life-limiting or terminal illnesses in Oxfordshire. They also provide equipment for children, which can improve their day-to-day lives, and a counselling service for families who are affected by having a child who is suffering from an illness requiring respite care.

Contents

What is dying?

I am standing on the seashore, a ship sails in the morning breeze and starts for the ocean.

She is an object of beauty and I stand watching her till at last she fades on the horizon and someone at my side says, “She is gone.”

Gone!

Where?

Gone from my sight, that is all.

She is just as large in the masts, hulls and spars as she was when I saw her, and just as able to bear her load of living freight to its destination.

The diminished size and total loss of sight is in me, not in her, and just at the moment when someone at my side says,

“She is gone”,

there are others who are watching her coming,
and other voices take up a glad shout:
“There she comes!”
and that is dying.

The Ship, Bishop Charles Henry Brent

Prologue

From somewhere out of the haze, I heard my name being called.

"Joanna! Joanna!"

I looked up. I had my arms around Matthew, who, at the age of eight, was safely snuggled up, asleep on my lap.

"Joanna, you need to get up; we're going." David's face emerged through the fog of my grief.

The pallbearers were bringing her small coffin close to where we were sitting, and I knew I should be walking behind it with David. Waking Matthew as gently as possible, I whispered, "It's OK, it's OK; we need to go now."

Time was running out, and I wanted more than anything to be there behind her on her final journey. I held Matthew's hand in mine, making sure he was steady on his sleepy feet before we joined David and Ben, ready to walk together as a family behind our beloved Alice.

As we fell into step behind the coffin, I heard the explosion of cries: the outbreak of sadness from our friends and family, the gasps of grief. I felt I was being covered with a blanket of sorrow. But my tears were yet to fall; I was keeping all my emotions safely hidden away in a deep and private place. The pain I felt was overwhelming, but somehow I had found a way to keep it contained. If I let down my guard for even an instant, if I allowed myself to face the horror of that day, to give vent to my grief for just a moment, then I knew I would be utterly lost. If I let go and began to cry, I didn't know how I could ever bring myself back.

As I walked behind my daughter's body, I caught sight of Scarlet sitting in a pew to my right. I lightly took hold of her arm with a squeeze of acknowledgement and gratitude that she'd come. We didn't make eye contact, but that moment of closeness was enough. I carried on walking, every part of my body in pain. It felt like ice shards were digging into my belly, my back, my head, my heart.

The day that I'd dreaded was finally here and terrifyingly real.

I always knew I'd write about Alice eventually. But where would I begin, and how would I be able to tell her story? How could I accurately convey who she was? How would I enable those who had never met her to see the real and perfect her, trapped in an imperfect, and eventually fatal, body? Would I be able to make them fall in love with her just as everyone who met her had done? How could I accurately put into words that I knew her life had been planned, and that it all happened just as it was always meant to?

It was never going to be easy to portray Alice. For a start, she never spoke in any traditional language. She wasn't an easy child to describe – and yet she was always straightforward. Those who took the trouble and time to get to know her understood exactly who she was and what she was like. They seemed to know instinctively what she wanted without having to ask her, which would have been futile as she couldn't have explained anyway.

For every sentence I tried to write about Alice there were ten others that I crossed out, fifty more that I'd scribbled, a hundred spoken, a thousand mumbled, ten thousand thought of. But now, at last, is the time for me to start.

Alice never talked. She was nearly six when she died, but in reality (according to the doctors and educational specialists) she was similar in her mental development to a nine-month-old, although it's hard to be entirely accurate. Alice was severely disabled, which meant she was physically and mentally unable to figure out the building blocks that most of us can put in place subconsciously as we grow up. She never hit the tantrum stage of throwing a spoon full of lovingly cooked, home-made food onto the floor. She needed constant help. However, with the support of an exceptional paediatric physiotherapist and her family and friends, Alice eventually learnt to walk unaided.

We had some outstanding specialists – physiotherapists, occupational therapists, speech and language therapists. She was never able to toilet herself and never really fed herself. She couldn't even point to or indicate something she needed or wanted. The fact that she never seemed to want for anything is reassuring. The truth is that I knew Alice inside out, as did many of our carefully selected team who supported both my husband and mainly me, in what was, at the time, the unknown world of the chronically disabled.

Life was enough for Alice. She was happy with everything she was given, be it practical things or more elusive things, like love, humour and friendship. There was a reason why everyone who spent time with Alice was moved by her and grew to love her; it is hard to describe. I hope that by writing this book, I might unlock, or at least uncover, her secret treasure of peace and happiness; the infectious inner beauty that was Alice.

In some Jewish families, when there has been a death, the mirrors in the house are covered with a cloth, taken down, or turned around to face the wall. Although there are many different explanations for this, I now think it should be compulsory whatever the original intention.

Regrettably I didn't know about this custom. I didn't cover our mirrors or take them down, which meant, after Alice died, I repeatedly caught sight of myself in a state of ugly, gut-wrenching, tear-stained grief. Even more disturbing was the fact that I knew this was the image of their mother that my dearest sons, Ben and Matthew, must have seen every hour, every day, in the weeks and months following Alice's death.

One of my reasons for writing Alice's story now is that I feel I have a measure of clarity and peace that enables me to put some things down on paper. Hopefully, these words will help my boys to one day be able to make sense of that image of their mother's grief, their father's distraught bewilderment and their sister's sudden disappearance.

I don't know if or when Ben and Matthew will read this – maybe when they are old enough to understand what happened. In the very same breath I realise that neither of them, or even us, will ever be old enough to fully understand what we lived through in those six short years, what we experienced when we held Alice firmly and tenderly in the heart of our family, and then what we felt when we were forced to let her go.

So, here is the story of Ben and Matthew's perfect sister, Alice, entrusted to us – to all of us. I believe we were hand-picked; me, David, Ben and Matthew. This is also the story of how she was taken – not snatched, just gently and tenderly released from our collective and perplexed embrace.

Part One

1991–2000

1

Twenty-One Years Earlier

Twenty-one years before that life-shattering day when we buried our beloved Alice, I was in my early twenties and had just graduated from university. My mother was in remission from breast cancer, having been diagnosed the previous year, when she was forty-five. The news of her cancer had been a life-changing event for me. I was just nineteen when she was diagnosed. The family line had always been that "Fortunately it's been caught early, and it's OK because there is a lot they can do about breast cancer now." That was just about as far as the conversation went. None of us knew how to talk openly about it. I'm guessing that it was too frightening for my parents and, for my part, I became complicit in their secrecy and accepted that it would always be somewhat of a taboo subject.

I discovered later that Mum had sat on the information about the menacing lump in her breast for six months. She was a busy woman, working as the marketing director in my father's new publishing company, and she had deliberately chosen to wait until a more 'convenient' time to face reality and have the growth investigated. I wonder if she had forgotten that she had three dependent children, all of us still in our teens – me at nineteen, and my brothers close on my heels at seventeen and sixteen years old. I don't think she, like most of us, ever dreamt she could be at risk of the very worst happening.

Very soon after I was told that my mother had cancer, my life began to fall apart. I felt choked in a pitch-black nothingness and was devastatingly unhappy. I couldn't breathe, couldn't think, and I couldn't possibly imagine life without Mum at the helm, issuing commands and instructions. Her cheering and whispering her hopes and ideas about the wind and the waves of the future seas laid out for me were my food, my drink, my very breath. Studying for my degree held little importance now; it paled into insignificance beside my mother's illness, which might mean she wouldn't live to see me graduate, never mind to see my life evolve. I was never able to talk openly then, and I only learnt to do so a long time after she died.

She went through aggressive chemotherapy and radiotherapy for breast cancer, and then she had more treatment on her lymph nodes, to which the disease had thoughtlessly spread. She was given the 'Congratulations, you're in remission' talk by the doctors, and following my graduation, nearly two years after I found out she was ill, she suggested I take a year off.

Under her guidance and enthusiasm, I (she) had decided that I should take a gap year before the melee of adult work and real-life took over. I hadn't had a break before going on to university from school, and so she (evidently I) felt it was time for me to see the world.

The 'all-clear' meant we were now feeling hopeful about the future. We were able to plan the years together as a family. I worked as hard as I could for as many hours as I was able, to earn money to fund this sudden adventure abroad. I needed to buy my backpack as well as purchase (together with my travelling companion Jane) the ridiculously small and lightweight tent which was to house both of us. We had also budgeted a painfully inadequate $5 a day for food, accommodation, clothes, medication and all our travel expenses. This figure hardly seems possible, and certainly wouldn't be if we tried to survive on such a paltry sum today. As it turned out, I came back with my foreign money crumpled together with the now-useless coins clattering in my pockets. My gap year didn't exactly work out as planned.

At the time, I was a skinny, twenty-one-year-old fake blonde backpacking in South Africa, Zimbabwe, Malawi, Tanzania and Kenya, playing make-believe that life with Mum was never going to change. As it turned out, I only managed the first leg of my journey, and had to give up my plans to travel to the Far East and ultimately spend three months in India.

Before I left for my travels, my mother's older sister, my Aunt Marie-Louise, who was a 'born again' Christian, had given my mother a Bible to give to me. I had only just arrived in Africa when I received a letter from my mother explaining that she had wanted to give me a Bible before I left the UK. Somehow this hadn't happened, and she told me that she had sent it and asked me to watch out for it at various poste restante addresses. I hadn't asked for the Bible, but it was typical of my charming, energetic ballet dancer aunt to have given it to my mother to pass on to me.

Marie-Lou had carefully marked some relevant passages for me to read. My aunt was a whirlwind of enthusiasm, with wavy, bright gold hair that she managed to style elegantly throughout her life, even up until the very last and difficult few weeks before she died two years ago.

In my formative years, I had been brought up as a Catholic and attended a relatively rigid Catholic boarding school, St Mary's Ascot, in Berkshire. I'd struggled for years with faith – my faith; any faith. As a child and then as a young woman, I knew I wanted to know God, but I also knew, having been immersed in a convent, that I did not want to be a nun. This faith had seemed, in my limited experience, to be the only way to honestly know God and to be known by Him. At university, I did a joint honours degree in English and Philosophy and, amongst other subjects, I had chosen to study Philosophy of Religion and Moral Philosophy. I consciously knew that my heart was seeking answers to the mysteries of life, and when Mum became ill, my need for those answers became even more urgent. In her inimitable way, Marie-Louise had helped my mother to find the rudiments of faith, introducing her to the Bible, and now Mum felt it incumbent on her to help me find mine.

In Africa, Jane and I had already travelled to at least four countries before I received the Bible. I had met Jane, a beautiful brown-haired, green-eyed girl, at university, and she had become a good friend. My original digs on campus had been far from ideal. My mother had helped me move into the soulless 1960s building made mostly of breeze blocks, and it was cold accommodation in every grey, English way. Within weeks of joining the University of East Anglia, we'd suffered the infamous 1987 Michael Fish no-storm hurricane, which uprooted most of the trees outside my room and along many of the campus roads. Suddenly I heard that a place had become available in the house that Jane was living in, on Earlham Road in Norwich. I didn't know Jane particularly well; she was working hard studying Law and I was a little in awe of her. At that time, she was in her second year and I was only in my first term, but she and her friends took me in and gratefully I occupied a space in the house she shared with two others.

Neither Jane nor I are quite sure how we ended up as a travelling duo; however, after we had both graduated, we knew each other well enough to decide that eight or nine months together, away from the UK, was an excellent idea.

Before I received the Bible in Africa, I had been looking out for my mother's/Aunt Marie-Louise's parcel at the various letter stations on our travels, but I kept missing it. The more I missed it (or, rather, it missed me), the more I longed to have it. The more I tried to get it and failed, the more I wanted to see what was written in it. Every time I arrived at one of the post restante addresses, the Bible was either still travelling or had just been sent on to the next location, possibly because we often arrived earlier or later than planned.

The thought of this Bible became more and more intriguing. As I've grown older, I've learnt that whatever is denied me, I have always had to have. I don't think this trait is peculiar to me as it's undoubtedly a universal human trait. When I later became a Christian, I struggled with this aspect of free will. I'm not entirely sure at what point I received my aunt's Bible, but once I finally had it in my hands, I opened it and immediately started devouring it. My way of looking at life and my values began very subtly to change. Looking back, this was the time when my clear memories begin. Before this point, my recollections are tainted with hang-ups and my natural insecurities, peppered with the hedonistic years of school and university.

With the burden of my twenty-kilo backpack, as I travelled to dirty and unfamiliar cities, hitch-hiking in random cars around Africa, traipsing through scrubland and negotiating noisy bus stations, I kept thinking of Jesus walking to His death, carrying the cross He was going to be crucified on. I kept thinking, as I climbed Mount Nyangani in Zimbabwe (2,592 metres), and then Mount Mulanje in Malawi (three thousand metres), close to Blantyre, and then finally Mount Kenya (5,199 metres), that at least I was going to see something stunning that I had chosen to see, like a sunrise, rather than going to be crucified. I kept thinking how selfish I was, dwelling on my personal 'hardship' of carrying a cumbersome backpack rather than the splintering wooden cross which Jesus had hauled on His back. My own 'hardship' was a working backpack and a future that included food. My 'hardship' included walking while clothed and wearing clean underwear. I think my pathetic 'hardships' are sometimes humorously known as 'First World problems'.

Looking back, I'm sure my internal battleground could only have been sparked by reading the Bible. The literature in question was a *Bible in One Year* edition of the famous book. Marie-Louise had decorated the opening page with red hearts and golden stars, as well as copying some verses of the following psalm in her thick black italic pen. Anyone who has been the recipient of one of her birthday cards, a letter of condolence or encouragement, will recognise this description of her very individual, very italic, and decidedly black, ink-laden script. Here are some of the words she copied and highlighted for me:

PSALM 139 VS. 1–10

You have searched me, Lord,
and You know me.
You know when I sit and when I rise;
You perceive my thoughts from afar.
You discern my going out and my lying down;
You are familiar with all my ways.
Before a word is on my tongue,
You, Lord, know it completely.
You hem me in behind and before,
and You lay Your hand upon me.
Such knowledge is too wonderful for me,
too lofty for me to attain.
Where can I go from Your Spirit?
Where can I flee from Your presence?
If I go up to the heavens, You are there;
if I make my bed in the depths, You are there.
If I rise on the wings of the dawn,
if I settle on the far side of the sea,
even there Your hand will guide me,
Your right hand will hold me fast.

I memorised these verses, as the words spoke to me in a deep and very dark place. They proved very pertinent as I scaled mountains in Africa, watched crocodiles or hippos from our clapped-out boats, and trundled through some of the little-charted lands of my unexplored world.

The words about God knowing us, wherever we are, were unbelievably apt for me. I didn't know it then, but my mother would later ask, in her will, that I read this psalm at her funeral.

By the time I was in Kenya, my diary entries were about praying for others – for Jane, for the health of my mother – and for safety. Had anyone asked me, I would have undoubtedly denied that I had any belief in God; however, I can see now that a trust in Him was gradually becoming part of my everyday life.

My journey into genuine faith in Jesus started slowly – excruciatingly slowly. I have a vivid memory of being somewhere on a bus in Zimbabwe. (In Africa, we seemed to spend a lot of time on buses, travelling from one utterly gorgeous place to another.) I remember looking out of the filthy window at the dazzling country bathed in bright, perfectly clean, toasty hot sunshine. The vehicle that I was on was a stinking, rickety local machine, inside which, along with their owners, were squawking chickens, scrawny lambs, smelly goats and other beasts, on their way to be either sold, cooked or traded. I began thinking about Jesus and what I knew about the Scriptures from when I was at school, and I remember trying to speak to Him.

Rather irreverently, given the circumstances, I began a silent prayer. *OK, Jesus,* I said. *You said You were resurrected… You said You didn't die. Or, rather, that You died and You were resurrected.* I felt emboldened to carry on. *So, if this is true and You are alive, then You* can *speak to me today, which will prove that You are alive.* I paused. *The Resurrection is either a* lie *or it's* the truth, *and if it is the truth, then I don't want to miss out. I don't want to get to the end of my life and discover I've missed out on this whole thing. To find out I've missed out on You for most of my life. I want to know the truth. I don't care what it costs. I want to know You.*

In retrospect, this seems a rather idiotic thing to think, let alone to mentally say to Him, but I know I meant it, and now I know that He was faithful to my prayer.

In the Bible, as I learned later, Jesus said, "Whoever wants to save his life will lose it, but whoever loses his life for my sake will find it, because what profit will a person have if he gains the whole world and forfeits his life? Or what can a person give in exchange for his life?" (Matthew 16:26)

I would far rather have chosen to 'lose my life' than to have lost my daughter without Him.

It's not a surprise that nothing happened that day on the bus in Zimbabwe. I had no idea until I got back to England that God was answering my prayers. I quite simply had no idea how silently and carefully He was working with me.

One of the mysteries of faith, certainly for me, is that I chose to trust in something or someone that I had hoped for, but had no idea was true.

2

The Returning

After we left Africa, we travelled a little through Asia, passing through Sumatra, Indonesia and Thailand on our way to India. I had left a comprehensive list of everywhere we were planning to stay and one night my father caught up with me. For once we happened to be in the right place at the right time. He called me at the C&C guest house in Bangkok. I remember taking the phone from the owner, whose hands smelled of garlic and raw meat. My father's voice wobbled over the line from hazy, forgotten England.

"You need to come home. Mummy's cancer has spread; she's not well."

I was devastated. I knew that things had suddenly and fundamentally changed, and I hurriedly packed what little

I had with me into my worn, sandy and smelly backpack and found a flight as quickly as was humanly possible. I cut my trip short by four months while Jane stoically carried on to India alone. She never complained or felt sorry for herself. I have only ever heard minor details of Jane's time in India, and she was incredibly gracious, given that this was meant to be our chance of freedom together, exploring and enjoying all that the world has to offer.

It was a shame that Jane was left on her own, and a shame for me too that I had to learn at such a young age just how tragic life could be. I boarded the plane feeling as if my world had been torn apart, ripped into shreds and then thrown malevolently into my face. I'd been travelling and having fun, with my whole life like an unopened flower bud ahead of me. It was such a shocking contrast to be returning to the UK, not yet knowing that I was soon going to be with my very sick, heartbroken, dying mother. Even though she had been ill for two years, this was something I'd never thought conceivable, even in my worst and most graphic nightmares.

When I arrived home to our house in Berkshire, and I saw Mum, I realised that she had already gone. My vivid memory of joyfully waving goodbye to her from the car taking us to the airport, departed just as I had on the plane. Her beaming at me, as if her life was going to run alongside mine on my travels, haunted me. She was no longer my mother; she was somebody I had to care for, and virtually a stranger. She was absorbed by pain, and she was angry. It was hard to be at home alone, looking after her. After all, hadn't it always been her job to look after me? Now the tables had been abruptly turned I felt deserted, and found it hard to cope.

Mum padded around the house in her threadbare dressing gown with its faded printed flowers. Sometimes she absent-mindedly strayed into the garden to smell a rose or two. Other times she might hesitantly settle in front of the television in search of any kind anaesthesia for her pain. Often I'd sit by her side, holding her hand, stroking her fingers, examining her nails and smelling the exclusive fragrance that came just from her. Always knowing that one day this would be forgotten and that this day might be the very last time I'd be with her like this.

I did my best to shield her from the impact this torture was having on my life. I had an agonising lump in my throat as I tried to bury the horrifying thoughts and the fear of her death that was now becoming more and more inevitable. At times I could hardly breathe. Mummy alternated between dozing, crying and singing. The recurrent tune was an adulterated version of Elaine Paige's song, 'Memory' – *Midnight, not a sound from the pavement. Has the moon lost her memory? She is smiling alone…* But instead of these words mummy sang, "Memories, all I'm left with are memories…" and then, ironically, she couldn't remember any of the rest of the words, so she sang that one misquoted line over and over again.

I was a young and vulnerable twenty-one-year-old and had no idea what it meant to look after somebody, let alone my own mother. My memories of my time in Africa were already fading, together with my tan.

On one particular day, the Macmillan nurse, who had just examined my mother during a routine visit, told me that the cancer had spread to Mum's brain and that there was nothing more that could be done for her.

I fell into a desperate, hysterical panic. I had to find a way to stop this happening. I was alarmed that she might die in a matter of weeks, or possibly days, and then I wondered if it could happen right now. Should I call my overworked and distraught father to ask him to drive home from London? Should I call him to take him away from work and ask him to hurry back to say goodbye to his wife, my mother, right this instant? I would typically go to my mother to discuss any problem I was having. In a stiff body punch of reality, I realised that this was no longer an option.

Too late I realised that I should have talked this over with the nurse, but she had pulled the pin and thrown the grenade, and, as the fire raged, she left me with no number to call. I paced the house, stopping in the kitchen to mix the usual meal of plain custard for my mother. She would barely eat this, and then later go into her bathroom to retch and vomit up what little of it had made its way into her stomach. I often sat outside her room and silently sobbed as I heard my darling mother gagging and coughing, then spitting out her paltry meal. I felt like doing the same with the nurse's statement about Mum's deteriorating health. I was desperate knowing that the cancer had spread and there was nothing more to be done for her. Terrified, yet needing to cope, I'd never before felt so isolated.

Marie-Louise came to stay that evening. My elegant aunt, who had metaphorically chased me around Africa with the Bible, arrived with no other agenda than seeing her sister and helping me out for a few days. As soon as my mother, my dying mother, had gone to bed, I spluttered out the nurse's assessment. Marie-Louise and I sat together at the kitchen table, staring into the chronic abyss. While I talked about the recent news, she remained uncharacteristically quiet, then said, "When I was as desperate as you are now, I just had to put my trust in God."

I can't remember how long it was before I left to go upstairs. All I remember after this is feeling a kind of peace that I hadn't felt since I'd first found out about Mum's cancer. I remember climbing into bed, turning off the light, and sleeping dreamlessly for a rare, full, uninterrupted night.

I woke the following morning in a state of ecstasy. It was the kind of elation that only a teenager might understand – the excitement before going to see a favourite band in concert, or going on a first date. I jumped out of bed, knowing that the Bible was true. It was as if all its words had been written on my heart. I suddenly knew that the Bible is the Word of God, that Jesus is alive and would be with me forever. Twenty-nine years later, this feeling is stronger than ever.

I called my then-boyfriend, expecting to be able to share this news with him; presuming he also knew what I now knew. In my mind's eye, everyone else was also aware of all that I was now aware of, as it seemed so blatantly obvious to me.

His voice was deadpan as he answered, "Oh, really?"

I realised at that precise moment that the whole world had not changed. It was, in fact, just me. So, I was on my own again, and yet now, never alone, always with Jesus.

It was not long after this happened that my mother, who fiercely wanted my brothers and me to find a belief in God, and for us all to know what eternal life meant, arranged with Marie-Louise to buy us some tickets for a Christian camp. We dutifully did everything that she wanted us to do, and we all obediently stayed in our unglamorous tents alongside two thousand other teenagers doing the same. I was intrigued by the whole set-up; my brothers less so. We listened to talks mostly aimed at teenagers about topics that were relevant to them. I was a little older, but they spoke to me too. Talks that told us who Jesus is and what it meant to be a Christian, and we heard bands and listened to Christian music around camp fires in the evenings. We watched the other young during the group events and around the campsite. It was a very different kind of Glastonbury experience.

This was where both my brothers found faith and hope in Jesus. As soon as I rang Mum from the camp to tell her that we had all now made a genuine commitment to God, her lung collapsed, and she was rushed to hospital.

She died two weeks later. It was as if she felt safe knowing that we had all found a belief in God, and we each had our own knowledge of an eternal future. It's hard not to think that she had been waiting for this to happen before she would let go and die.

So, it hadn't only been Marie-Louise's Bible that brought about my conversion to Christianity. It wasn't only my prayer on the bus, or even my conversation with my aunt in my parents' kitchen.

It was a mixture of a heart that was desperate and ready, and a God who is able.

3

The Promise

Less than a year into my newly found belief, I realised I wanted to understand why and how I believed in Jesus and, most importantly, who He was. I'd come to Christianity relatively quickly and, soon after, I signed up to do a year at Bible college, which was generously paid for by my father.

After my mother had died, I had rashly given up a potential career in film, television and possibly radio, having been a runner in many production companies during most of my school and university holidays. I had worked briefly at the BBC and, while at university, on the news desk, even cutting my own news pieces at Radio Broadland in Norwich. Until this point I had felt I had a life plan in place and was excited about the potential future ahead of me. I had recently split up with my boyfriend, and then suddenly, seemingly out of nowhere, I found myself studying the Bible and living in my father's flat in London, questioning absolutely everything. If my future wasn't going to be in television production or radio any more, and nothing else looked the same, then I wanted to know what on earth I was going to do with my life.

One day, seven months after I had 'discovered' Jesus, I was at home. I had spent a long morning praying and fervently asking God to speak to me. I wanted to know the answer to my life's purpose and function. I didn't feel I had anyone to turn to, and I desperately wanted to know where my life was heading.

On this day I had a dramatic experience. After over an hour of intense prayer, I felt God give me some verses from the Bible; verses which were taken totally out of context, but words that I felt Him speak specifically to me. Frankly, I would have taken anything. I was young, had only recently lost my mother, who had been the director of all my operations, and I felt like a boat without a sail, adrift on the open sea. I longed to know what my new future held. I'm not sure whether this was the result of insecurity, or a need to control. It could have been either or both as I can't honestly remember who I was then.

The initial thing I 'heard' after I had prayed was *Zechariah 7:4*:

> Thus the word of the Lord came to me, saying...

I was quite freaked out; it felt so random. That is all that's said in this verse. It seemed to say to me, *I'm listening; watch what I am going to say to you…*

Looking back, I might have thought that I had heard God say, *Hezekiah 20:7*, which says:

> Then Isaiah said, "Prepare a poultice of figs." They did so and applied it to the boil, and he recovered.

Funny. It could have been any one of the over thirty-one thousand verses that make up the Bible, most of which would no doubt have ended up being utterly irrelevant to me. I might have thought I heard Him say, *Proverbs 31:6* ('Let beer be for those who are perishing, wine for those who are in anguish!'), which might have been more useful to someone in their twenties.

If either of these had been the case, then I wouldn't have looked any further, and I would have dropped all my questioning. I wasn't able to let go because of this first, very striking verse. I kept asking, and then turning to the passages that seemed to be speaking to me. There were fifty-six verses taken from ten different chapters in a total of four books in the Bible that spoke to me on that morning. At the end of the time I spent praying, I felt led to a chapter that told me it was finished. I felt Him say, *Deuteronomy 32:46–47*. Which reads:

> Take to heart all the words by which I am warning you today, that you may

> command them to your children, that they may be careful to do all the words of this law. They are not just idle words for you – they are your life. By them you will live long in the land you are crossing the Jordan to possess.

I didn't feel the need to take any of what I had recorded literally, and I still have no idea what to 'live long in the land you are crossing the Jordan to possess' could mean for me. What I can take from what was said to me has been enough. The fact that I recorded all He apparently said to me in 1992 illustrates that there was no doubt in my mind of its relevance. I typed up and kept these verses very safe, not yet understanding how they were pertinent to my life. I genuinely knew I had experienced something extraordinary, but also that I had no idea what any of it meant.

What it does mean today, is that I am sitting here ridiculously writing this account of my daughter's short and extraordinary life.

4

A New Way Forward

It was another seven years before I met David, and at the time, I had decided that marriage was not going to be a realistic or even a sensible option for me.

I had been diagnosed with multiple sclerosis when I was twenty-four, three years after I had lost my mother, and this illness had begun to dominate my life. At the time of my diagnosis, I had been genuinely ill. I had a serious loss of balance as well as loss of sight in my right eye, and what little vision I had was disrupted by double vision. I also had chronic tingling in my whole body, which was heightened by a loss of feeling in my fingers and toes. The list of symptoms was inexhaustible, and made worse by finding out, from my GP, who took an active interest in neurological illnesses, that my earliest episodes had probably occurred in my mid teens. These had always been put down by the school medics to trapped nerves following exercise. My illness had come on relatively suddenly, and with the severity of my symptoms, I now thought I probably wouldn't live to see my thirtieth birthday.

After I was diagnosed with MS and it had been confirmed by an MRI, I had been put on a course of intravenous steroids, and I went on an exhaustive hunt for ways to change my lifestyle and habits. Back in the day when I first had MS, the traditional medics didn't know if this illness was due to an underactive immune system or an overactive one, and there were few drugs to help treat the sickness in the long term. So, I stopped smoking and drinking, and went on a diet that contained more fruit and vegetables than meat and chips. I recovered from all of my so-called 'attacks', my eyesight and balance were restored, and the numbness in my digits was gone. This 'alternative therapy' knowledge was invaluable when I struggled with my daughter's heath and her lack of a diagnosis.

By the time I met my warm-eyed, dark-haired and somewhat mysterious husband, I was mostly back to good health. This didn't mean, however, that I was hoping to get married. I was still expecting to be single, but David had other plans. Even though I told him I had MS, that

I didn't think I was going to have children, and what I wanted was to work with orphans in Africa, he listened and told me he would wait for me and support me in anything I decided to do.

Whatever I said didn't stop him tenaciously lifting me off the shelf, dusting me off and sweeping me off my feet. We were both twenty-nine when we met, and we were engaged within six weeks, despite the fact that we'd only met seven times. Either I wasn't committed to my no-marriage policy or my knees had weakened spectacularly.

And now here I am, at the time my story of Alice begins, sixteen years after my powerful experience of discovering my faith in God – a happy wife, married to David, and a mother of three beautiful young children. Our life was on the road that most of us walk down, some drive on, and occasionally others have the privilege of flying over.

We were now living in London in a rented basement flat in Pimlico. David was working for a venture capital firm round the corner, which he had joined just after we returned from our honeymoon. Six months into marriage, I fell pregnant and we went enthusiastically to the NCT classes, me reading all the books I could find to discover what was happening inside my body. During this emotional period, David declared to me that he didn't feel he was going to be able to be present at the birth!

We were both thirty when we married, which meant that we had already clocked up a considerable amount of decision-making time in the relative calm of being single. We were now, however, trying to find our feet as a couple. Quietly and mostly subconsciously, we were both individually trying to work out the unwritten rule book, the guide to marriage for the uninitiated. For us, this questionable guide seemed to be in another language or never available when we needed it. David's revelation that he was afraid of blood and became quite faint when confronted with it did not appear to be in my copy of the book.

In the event, he stayed close by my side for most of the sixteen hours of my first labour. Given what happened at my next two births, 'the universe', 'the higher power' or, as I see it, our God, must have an exotic sense of humour. After sixteen hours of intense labour, Ben, our patient, kind, thoughtful, cricket-mad schoolboy opening batsman son, arrived.

Naturally, for our second child, I was hoping for a quicker labour, yet at the same time anticipating a repeat of the first birth. Matthew was expected a traditional two years after our first and, as by that time we were living in Hampshire, Basingstoke Hospital seemed the sensible option for the birth.

The morning Matthew was born was during a sweltering summer, and even when we left for the hospital from our farmhouse at half six in the morning, I knew it was going to be another scorcher. The hospital was a thirty-minute drive away, and things were moving fast before we even set off. I had refused the cup of tea David had offered me before we left. As we stood at the front door, he appeared to be bizarrely preoccupied in a conversation about golf, and specifically Huntercombe, the local golf club, with my father, who had generously offered to stay at home and take care of Ben for us.

Despite my attempts to convey to David that we needed to get going as I was in labour – "Darling, we need to go… *now*!" – he remained, in my view, catatonically relaxed.

Eventually, he got the message, and as we sped along the road to Basingstoke Hospital, I remember gripping the armrests and trying to 'breathe through' the contractions. David sensibly ignored my ridiculous requests to pull over so that I could control the contractions. Seconds before we turned into the hospital grounds, my waters broke. I couldn't bring myself to make eye contact with the driver of a lorry that we were stuck beside at the traffic lights outside the hospital.

As my waters broke, I was still trying to clarify the details of 'our' birthing plan with David. I had a list of essential information, like where to park the car, where the change was to be found to put in the parking meter and, not least, what exactly the maternity team needed to know about me wanting a water birth!

As we pulled into the car park, I realised there was no way I'd be able to walk the short distance to the hospital entrance. I asked David to stop at the drop-off point by the door to Accident & Emergency, the one usually reserved for ambulances. He drew the car up reluctantly and, with a subtle shrug of his shoulders as he got out, told me that he "really shouldn't be doing this". As he reached the intercom and called for the midwives to come down, I suddenly had a strange sensation in my nether regions. I put my hand between my legs and, through the light material of my shorts, could feel a hardness that was unmistakably not part of me. I yanked off my shorts.

"David!" I screamed out of the window. "I can feel the head!"

David spun round to be greeted with the alarming sight of his wife half-naked in the passenger seat of the car, her shorts wrapped around her ankles, the car door ajar and goodness knows what else on show to the world. He told me later that all he could think was, *What on earth is my wife doing taking her shorts off?*

He rushed back, knelt on the pavement beside the passenger seat, and caught the baby. This all happened in a matter of seconds. Seconds jam-packed with astonishment, delight and shock. We had a baby that we had delivered together! And it had happened in our now-soiled car in a fairly grotty car park.

The midwives came rushing down from the ward in a whirlwind of uncharacteristically curt comments.

"Sorry I didn't call," I mumbled, and, "No, I'm afraid I don't have a towel", and "No! I also don't have a baby blanket to hand."

The ordinarily good-natured midwives looked at me with consternation as I tried to assure them that we hadn't planned for this to happen. Surely I wasn't the first expectant mum to give birth in the hospital car park? Yet, it seemed that perhaps I was. After minutes of labour, many evenings of excruciating Braxton Hicks contractions, Matthew our dynamic, cricket-indoctrinated schoolboy opening bowler son, clearly couldn't wait to join us.

5

Kids at Home

I now had two healthy, bubbly boys: one brown-haired and warm-brown-eyed; the other blond and brilliant-blue-eyed. I was in my early thirties, pretending and feeling like I was still in my twenties. Before I fell pregnant with Alice, I'd decided that my two boys were enough for me. I could fully enjoy them, instruct them, try to entertain them, administer plasters and bandages, and dose them up with Calpol or Nurofen if and when necessary. I also had a Jack Russell. I'd bought this puppy in a hasty moment from a dear friend of my mother's, Julie, who had become a very close friend of mine too. Her puppy, now mine, was a young minx of a terrier and was an ample third 'child'.

We didn't live far from David's parents, and when we were all able, it was lovely to share our lives intergenerationally! When Anthony, David's father, got dressed in the morning, he never forgot to put on his smile and wear his laughter. Both he and Anne, David's mother, loved spending time with us, and always brought edible or drinkable gifts for us as well as treats for the two boys. Anthony was a very unusual man, his bright eyes were lit with love and life, and he was a genuine strength to me. My life was feeling full and 'ordered' and everything was speeding along on a traditional route. Work-wise, David was not on a conventional road; he was now self-employed and fighting to keep us all fed, clothed and watered. He managed this pressure without ever complaining and with huge determination.

Ben and Matthew were growing and changing rapidly. They both have August birthdays, which means they are always the youngest in their school year. Because Ben had never been to nursery, I made sure that, before he started school, he had had several 'play dates' with children who would be in his class. He'd been well rehearsed. I'd introduced him to some of his peers, and he'd been to others' houses as he made new friends. I was getting to know the young mums and he the younger children.

Our neighbours had three children. The two youngest, Nick and Emma, spent many hours at our house, playing in the garden, or pushing Ben in a wheelbarrow around the farm where we lived. Eating crisps and devouring chocolate cake and jellies on birthdays, there was lots of laughter and fun in those days. When the time came for

Ben to go to school, Nick and Emma made cards wishing him good luck for his first day. They appeared at our door, dressed smartly in their school uniforms, clasping the envelopes in their hands and sporting enthusiastic grins. They were thrilled that Ben was starting school, and I thought he was as ready as I could have hoped for.

On the day he was due to start school, Ben ate his porridge hesitantly, a meal usually consumed with gusto. That first day, when David and I set off in the car with Ben in the back, leaving Mathew at home with a nanny, Ben seemed calm as he stared out of the window. We drove through the narrow, winding country lanes leading up to the small, friendly preschool. The junior classroom was located in a barn hidden by the side of the school the older children attended.

Together, David and I, with Ben in the middle, walked along the path leading to the barn, past climbing frames, slides and a cheerful playground painted with numbers, patterns and animals, with plastic shapes to jump in and out of. We, or rather I, chatted cheerfully about the morning Ben was going to spend with his new friends, Douglas, George and Julian. I said that I was going to go shopping for some bits and bobs for supper and would be back by lunchtime, when I would scoop him up to take him home for lunch.

Once Ben was in his classroom, David and I began to make our subtle escape. While we had a friendly chat with his teacher, ironically called Mrs Cope, I could tell Ben was getting nervous. He kept glancing up at me and looking at the door. As we moved towards the exit, he clutched my arm and wouldn't let go. It was a fairly traumatic time for David and me, as well as for Ben!

We managed to leave, and as we drove slowly through the school gates, we were stopped by another previously distressed mum on foot, who motioned to us that she wanted to have a word. I put down my window. With a grin, she leant in towards us and said, "Really, take heart – I persevered for a year with my son's dislike of school. Your little boy will settle eventually. William's fine now!"

I found out later that this was the point at which David's heart snapped. "A whole year!" he said when we were home. "I'm not putting my son through that for a whole year!"

I picked Ben up at lunchtime, so he hadn't been there too long. He had very little to say about his morning, and I said nothing about the potential evacuation plan I'd been discussing with his father.

The following day was worse. It was as if Ben had already begun to quietly shut down. David wasn't with me, and I said goodbye to Ben and left the classroom swiftly, not wanting the trauma of feeling my child trying to grab hold of my hand again. As I walked away, I heard my son's unmistakable cry and the confusion growing in his voice as he realised he was being left once more.

Thinking back, I'm sure he would have grown out of this fear, but how long would that have taken? Meanwhile, I was subjected to the sound of his anguish. I stood outside the little barn, with its black wooden boarding which I'd previously seen as quaint, but now saw as menacing. At that moment, I called on my faith, as I had done over the years in times of trouble. I prayed that I would be shown how this was the very best thing for Ben. As I silently wept, unseen, outside the school, I prayed that if this, though hard, were the best start for him, then I would have the strength to cope. I had given birth four years earlier to this incredible, enchanting child and I felt it was my responsibility to care for him as best I could, sparing no pain on my part, but putting his needs first.

I asked God, *What good can this do? How can this be a good thing for him? Please show me that this is the right thing to do for him. If it's not a good thing for him, for now, then help me know what to do.*

I must have stood outside Ben's school, crying and metaphorically wringing my hands, for nearly an hour before dragging myself away, when all I wanted to do was rush back in and gather him up. I drove to the supermarket, and while the tills rang out and beeped and buzzed their way through the start and end of the lines and lines of fresh fruit and vegetables, cans and cereals, household items and other essentials on people's shopping lists for the day, I called David.

"David, I can't do this," I spluttered. "Please, can I bring Ben home to stay, at least for the moment?" Between the humming and the bleeps of the electronic tallies, I mumbled, "Maybe I could teach him at home? Anything would be better than this." I explained how he'd been that morning and how unbearable it was.

"Yes, of course. Tell him he doesn't need to go back to school for now. Tell him we love him." There was a pause. "Are you sure you're ready to do this?" he asked.

The supermarket noises might have gone silent, but I didn't notice. The relief I felt when David agreed with me was overwhelming, and I couldn't wait to go and collect Ben. Only now can I see that perhaps this was another way I was being prepared for the difficult decisions I would have to make when I looked after Alice.

I arrived back at the school in a whirlwind of secret excitement streaked with panic. And that is how I came to homeschool Ben at the age of four. By the time he was eight-and-a-half, when he finally went back into mainstream schooling, he was completely ready. Long gone was his fear of separation; his transition to school worked smoothly and happily. When the time came, we discussed the school option, and he was confident. Matthew was probably not quite as ready, but sadly, by then, I no longer had a choice

6

London

After Ben's aborted schooling fiasco, we were looking at reassessing his situation on a termly basis. My grandfather had unexpectedly died at the beginning of the summer, and we had moved temporarily to Rutland to be near my newly widowed grandmother. We lived near her for roughly eight months, then returned to the South only because of David's demanding work commitments. His alarm had consistently rung out the need to go to London at an appalling hour in the morning. Now the nights were drawing in, and the winding, unlit single-track roads were becoming dangerously icy. So we moved, and it was while we were living in London that I unexpectedly fell pregnant with Alice.

Matthew, now a little over two, and Ben, just over four, were spending their days mucking about in mud and sand as we all explored the wonders of a carefree childhood. We were living close to Holland Park, and we enjoyed the gardens, the boys cycling up and down the slopes, giggling while watching our dog, Scally, fruitlessly chasing the cheeky squirrels. The obscene frogspawn erupting in the pond at the top of one of the hills delighted and revolted the boys in equal measure. I had spent a good deal of my childhood here, so it was amazing to share the very same places with my children.

It was during one of these days, in the glow of the soft light in our basement bathroom, after a morning spent with the boys, that I stared open-mouthed at the pregnancy test kit I'd bought the day before. It wasn't possible! Given my slightly compromised health issues, I had shied away from conventional birth control, not wanting to stress my system with unnecessary drugs, and had opted for a natural hormone tracking system. This method of contraception suited me very well, given that I was regular as clockwork – or, should I say, up until then it had worked perfectly. The only risk I now realise I'd taken was to spend a week during the previous month in the company of two pregnant women, which had caused my hormones to fly into an uncharacteristic flurry of confusion. My body had decided that I needed another baby! This is one of the mysteries regarding women's bodies. It seemed that mine just wanted to join in with the pregnancy party.

I attempted to adjust to the idea of having a baby that was neither planned nor, if I am honest, really wanted. Over the next few weeks, I tried to feel happy about the incredible privilege of being able to fall pregnant again, but I wasn't pleased, I wasn't thrilled, and I wasn't even remotely excited. I was struggling to impart kindness and joy to this minuscule new life inside me, but all I could hear in my heart was an empty clang and a questioning voice: *Is someone really meant to be in there?* I had to do at least three more tests to confirm that my fears were real. I was definitely pregnant.

One evening I was distractedly throwing together and cooking the ingredients for a Bolognese sauce: onions, mince, tomatoes, tomato sauce, tomato puree, a handful of spicy chillies, a spoonful of Lea & Perrins, a glug of red wine, garlic... had I remembered the garlic? My head was a muddle, and I found the heat and darkness of the basement London flat oppressive. Tears of confusion and frustration trickled down my cheeks as the boys happily mucked around in the room next door. Their books lay neatly stacked on the table. A frustrated mix of emotions welled inside my complicated heart. I didn't think I wanted another baby. Not only did I not want it, I felt sure I couldn't cope with another one.

F***! Not a word I use often, and not a word that I relish writing, but one that fitted my feelings at the time. It is also an ironic word given the circumstances. I toyed with the idea of three little voices filling my world instead of two, and I felt frightened. And yet, peculiarly, if I'm honest, very deep, deep down, I knew someone *was* meant to be there.

Several times in the past, I'd felt a spark of unfamiliar jealousy when I heard that there was a third child due to someone I knew. Where that unwelcome emotion came from, I had no idea. But now? Me? Really? This was not part of my neat, well-organised and fairly recently thought-out life plan. The indignation was overwhelming. I might have opened my legs and welcomed pleasure for an instant, but I didn't, at that moment, give my permission for a child, a life. Of course, I knew the risk, but naively I never dreamt this could or would ever happen.

Still, God had spoken to me very specifically prior to this happening, and has spoken to me over the years that have since passed. He has never stopped talking, although I admit I have often stopped listening. Here I was, about seven weeks after I discovered I was pregnant, in the tiny kitchen in our rented flat in Holland Park, stirring the boys' food just as this little being was starting to stir in my belly. I questioned God, lifting my tearful eyes to Him to ask for the hundredth time for some explanation for this unsought pregnancy. Then, as I saw the steam rise from the pasta and the Bolognese sauce bubble, I felt God clearly and intimately say to me, *This is My child; I carried it on the cross, it's Mine.*

To turn a cliché on its head, it was as if the world had suddenly started turning again. From that moment, I was filled with joy and a sense of trust mixed with abandon. I knew I had 'heard' the voice of God, and to this day, whenever I tell this story, I'm often moved to tears. I'd heard Him talking about Alice before she was born, claiming her as His own. I felt Him telling me that she had always been 'His child'.

A few days later, I once again turned to the verses I'd felt God give me when I was in my early twenties. These were shut up and nearly forgotten in a dusty book, which I always kept, now mostly unopened, close to where I slept. I now turned my full, undivided attention to them. Over the years, I had read and reread these passages, yet never understood what they might mean to me, but now, for the first time, I saw something real.

In the third set of the ten chapters I had recorded, I found Isaiah 44:3–5:

> For I will pour water on him who is thirsty,
> And floods on the dry ground;
> I will pour My Spirit on your descendants,
> And My blessing on your offspring;
> They will spring up among the grass
> Like willows by the watercourses.
> One will say, "I am the LORD's";
> Another will call himself by the name of Jacob;
> Another will write with his hand, 'The LORD's',
> And name himself by the name of Israel.

Suddenly this passage represented an obvious answer to my pregnancy turmoil. I recognised the voice, and I knew who had chosen this path for me. I realised that I had already been having these 'descendants' and 'offspring'. I'm not quite sure how I had missed the meaning behind these clear words. I felt at peace. If this was true for me, which I firmly believed it was, then I was meant to have three – not one, not two, but *three* – children. All my inexplicable feelings of jealousy about the third pregnancies around me now made more sense.

Ben was the offspring who said, "I am the LORD's"; then there was Matthew, 'who will call himself by the name of Jacob', and Alice: 'Another will write with his hand, "The LORD's", And name himself by the name of Israel.'

This seemed too extraordinary. In some random words in the Bible, given to me years before Alice was born, I saw something that spoke of my three children's births; it just seemed too incredible, in fact hardly credible.

At the time I recorded the words given to me, and for fourteen years after I first wrote down all the words I felt Him say, I had no understanding of what any of it meant. From time to time, I had read and reread those words, but they were still just words taken from a book; albeit an extraordinary book, but words that I felt had been given to me in exceptional circumstances.

It wasn't until I was pregnant with Alice that these words genuinely began to mean something compelling and life-altering to me, and it's interesting that He asked at the end of all the verses that I had copied down that day, for me to 'Take to heart' all the words that He was 'warning' me with that day.

Interesting that He mentions a warning. Perhaps I could have read more into this too.

Would I have chosen to have more children after Alice, once I knew the complexity of her situation, as well as a lack of diagnosis? Probably not. Having both the boys meant that I had a reason to continue, and they were and still are invaluable strengths to both David and me.

I remember talking to David and some of those closest to me; my cousin and very good friend Charlie, and Sheena, his wife. Also, I spoke to my dearest friend, Kay, whom I had met very soon after I'd had Ben. I hoped that perhaps one of them might be able to see what I could now see: that there was a purpose; that there was a plan. I remember describing how I had heard the words from God – *This is My child; I carried it on the cross, it's Mine.* Their reactions were stoically restrained, and wordlessly gracious.

Little did I know then, that on the day Alice died, the Lord's words would return to me. It was a day that proved to be a tragic affirmation that she had always belonged to Him.

And as it turned out, I gave back to Him the gift He'd so generously given me.

7

A Warning

I was adjusting to a new reality – another pregnancy and a third baby, one that was purposed.

We were still in London at the time of my twenty-week scan. We hadn't been in Holland Park long enough for me to have registered with my local GP practice, and frankly I wasn't expecting to need to because London hadn't seemed like a long-term option. Of course, I probably intended to find a doctor at some point, since I was responsible for two young boys, but the idea of joining anything that would suggest we were there permanently was not on my radar.

We were doing our very best to keep our fledgling family afloat wherever we happened to be. David was still working all hours, and I was doing the same with the children and the dog in tow. When we started talking about plans, we always felt drawn to the idea of returning to Rutland to be near my grandmother. We finally moved back to her neck of the woods when I was a nerve-racking eight months pregnant.

Before this big move, when we were still in London, and I was thirty-six years old, pregnant and the mother of two young boys, we visited a clinic in Harley Street for the pregnancy check-up. The boys weren't in school yet, we had no permanent place of residence and I didn't have a GP to look after me and the boys.

It's weird, looking back, trying to understand how we could ever have been trusted with children. Fortunately, no laws exist as yet that require one to qualify for parenthood. I remember my mother, years before she died, telling me that, as well as learning all the standard subjects at school, it should be mandatory to learn about parenthood. She found being a young mother very hard, a sentiment I'm sure many parents would share, particularly those with no hands-on parents of their own to help with the more demanding aspects. I certainly felt this.

At the scan, I remember being light-hearted and full of excitement about having another child. I had the words of His promise safely tucked away, along with the reference in Isaiah 44. David and I talked to the sonographer. I can't remember any details about him, or anything specific about the conversation we had. Still, I do remember hearing the words "potentially small baby" and "difficulties" and knowing that we were being given a choice to investigate a problem that he had spotted. We were told the baby might not grow properly; that it was possible it wouldn't thrive. Something was different with this third pregnancy, but we wouldn't know the specifics without an intrusive and potentially dangerous examination. Vague enough, but arresting enough too.

Before the sonographer had the chance to ask if we would ever consider an abortion, we made it as clear as clear can ever be that having an abortion was never going to be an option for us. He also mentioned my age and implied that, at thirty-six, I was an older mother. David and I have since discussed this day and know that he saw something, either in my blood or urine, or on the scan, that he was genuinely uneasy about, but we had shut him down very quickly.

Looking back, of course, I wish I'd responded differently and asked him what he meant and what it was, specifically, that was worrying him. We did know he was asking us to have in vitro tests that might have been damaging to our baby, but perhaps I should have asked him precisely what it was that wasn't normal. Might further investigation have meant that we could have done something more for Alice?

Whatever the rights and wrongs (probably wrongs), we both felt very strongly that we didn't want to know. This baby was meant to be, and from my point of view, I thought, *I don't care about any of these vague problems. This is the child I want. This child is determined.* Please excuse the deliberate pun – Alice was a very determined little girl.

We went back to the clinic years later, when it was clear that Alice was developmentally delayed, to see if we could find any information or records of what was said to us during that twenty-week scan. Any notes that may have existed had been destroyed, and the sonographer who spotted this abnormality in our baby seemed to have vanished. In fact, I'm guessing he didn't record any of our conversation. If he did destroy the notes, or even not make the notes in the first place, it was probably to protect himself, if not also to protect us.

I don't remember how the sonographer reacted to our unwillingness to entertain his concerns, although he was undoubtedly respectful and polite. I only know that there's nothing recorded about our consultation, which made things difficult later on. It also makes writing this tough because we have no concrete evidence of what was said at that point in the pregnancy.

It seemed as if everything was hidden from us from the start, and even after Alice's dying day. She left us with no anchors, no plan, no purpose, no understandable goal and, sadly, no apparent reason for her short life.

Maybe I'm right to blame myself. Why didn't I ask more questions in that room when I had the scan? Why didn't I probe more, or want to know more? Knowing that there was something wrong surely wouldn't mean I would be forced to make a decision that I didn't want to make. Still, I don't see any point in agonising about what I did or didn't do. At the time, I didn't ask, so that's that. Everything else about my pregnancy went very smoothly and, until about a year after Alice's birth, I all but forgot about the conversation we had at my twenty-week scan.

By the time I was eight months pregnant with Alice, we were back in Rutland, three years on from the incident with Matthew's arrival in Basingstoke Hospital car park. After my two previous experiences of giving birth, particularly the last one, I made sure I had a home birth organised for the new arrival. The large bottles of gas and air – which I was looking forward to using – were ready in our bedroom. Sadly, due to poor visibility on the roads the night that Alice arrived, the maternity nurse was late, and David ended up delivering baby number three as well! He coped exceptionally well with his fear of blood. His worry about being present at Ben's birth had become a distant memory after the arrival of Matthew in the car, and was soon eclipsed by the delivery of Alice.

This is just a word to the wise: be careful with the lines you draw in the sands of your life. Who is it that is really in control of our lives?

Part Two

2006–2009

8

The Arrival

I had never really wanted a girl, but was overjoyed the moment I knew. The midwife, who had sped into the house at the twelfth hour (having just missed the eleventh), took over from a shell-shocked David and confirmed that we had a girl.

Alice was a perfect healthy weight at 8lb 7oz and looked adorable in every way. Her eyes were, unusually for a newborn, already a warm hazel colour and she had a sweet covering of brown baby hair on her head. Over the next few months, her eyes became a dark, warm brown, like her father's and her brother Ben's. The murmur from the sonographer about a "small baby" could now be firmly laid to rest.

All of us loved Alice from the minute she arrived until the day she left. I can honestly say I never once had to reprimand her and never resented going into her room to settle her, no matter what the hour or how exhausted I was. This is more a testimony to her innate goodness and purity than my own restraint.

Her only blemish was a red mark on her ring finger. It looked to me as though it represented a kiss. These reasonably common marks on newborns are known as 'salmon patches' or, more colloquially, 'stork bites', and usually appear around the head and face. They are made up of small blood vessels (capillaries) and are visible through the skin.

I'd seen quite a few children with these birthmarks at various mother and toddler groups; however, the location of Alice's mark made me wonder. How strange that it should be on her wedding ring finger. It brought to my memory the comment that had changed my whole attitude to my pregnancy; that this child was God's child, that He had carried it on the cross and it was His. The birthmark seemed to mark her as belonging to God, and in my mind, to set her apart from our other two children.

I remember talking to Kay and telling her that I felt that this child was mine for as long as she still had that mark. I would frequently confide in Kay, who is wise and caring and never judged me. I first met her through my South African maternity nurse, and we kept in touch through everything. She became Alice's godmother, and I can honestly say I have never had a better or more genuine friend. I would do anything for her, as would my husband

and both my sons. I feel fortunate to have met her and that she joined our family. I might have lost my mother, but Kay became a wonderful substitute mother figure for me.

I felt very comfortable asking, and indeed telling, Kay anything. It was a peculiar thing for me to think that I might only have Alice for a while, and even stranger for me to put those thoughts into words. But I mentioned this to Kay long before there were any difficulties with Alice. As time passed, the birthmark became smaller and harder to see, which made me almost forget about the ridiculous assumption I'd made. I said this long before Alice started having seizures and even before there was any question that she might be developmentally delayed.

Remarkably, it wasn't until she was in hospital towards the end of her life that I thought back to my original foreboding about the stork bite on her ring finger. This child was mine for as long as she still had that mark. It was then that I took her delicate fourth finger on her left hand and played with it, gently touching it, studying it, all the while hoping that I could still make out a glimpse of the red capillaries that marked it. They were no longer visible.

I thought I'd kept my thoughts about her curious mark to myself, but Kay reminded me, after Alice died, that I had told her of my foreboding. I have discovered that, just like a mother, Kay has a shocking ability to sneak into my heart when I think it is only me and my private thoughts in there. She has always given me perfectly good reasons to trust her. Even now, I continually call her for her wisdom and guidance.

Another woman who played a vital role in our family when we'd just moved to Rutland was Janet. She had a thick, vibrant shock of golden hair and a huge grin to match her striking operatic voice. When I first met Janet, she was working as a temporary housekeeper for a neighbour of ours, having also worked with the previous owners of our new house. When we moved in, she popped round unannounced to introduce herself and to offer her services to me as a general home help.

Janet immediately struck me as someone I could trust and whose company I would enjoy. She had the most fantastic booming voice, and her laughter seemed to fill the room with light. She was the mother of two girls who had both left university, and one was engaged to be married. She always enthralled me with her desire never to be defeated by any problem, big or small, and she kept us entertained, regularly regaling us with extraordinary tales that could have come straight from the pages of a Jane Austen novel, or a Jeeves and Wooster story.

Janet seemed to have abilities that could flip age, ability or gender on their heads. Once when she was working for us she moved a double bed, mattress included, on her own, from an upstairs room to the floor below using nothing more than a home-made 'hay mover' trolley on two wheels. There was no damage to the walls or anything else, and she never even resorted to chucking the bed out of the window! I still don't quite know how she managed this.

Janet knew Alice from birth and always enjoyed being with her and singing to her. We didn't, of course, realise that there was anything wrong with Alice in those early days, and as the mother of two healthy young women, Janet always challenged me as to the best way to bring up a little girl.

She often took one of the boys to ride on Benny, one of the three horses that she looked after. Early on, I remember sitting in my freezing car near Janet's manège, feeding Alice while Janet skilfully threw Matthew onto the back of another of her horses, a gigantic seventeen-hand horse to take him riding. His tiny three-year-old body swayed precariously to the rhythm of the horse's great, languorous movement, as Janet led it along the path beside the manège. I watched him nervously in the rear-view mirror, a smaller and smaller dot in the distance, which I could barely pick out once the figure had dipped out of the reflection in my mirror. I desperately wanted to jump out of the car and at least put my hand protectively on his back, but I had a baby glued to my breast.

One of Matthew's favourite pastimes was asking Janet's huge cherry blonde Lurcher, Toby, to sit. He would then dig deep into his pockets while Toby would wait patiently for the biscuit to be posted into his waiting mouth. Matthew was the same height standing up as Toby was sitting down, Ben was only marginally taller!

A few years later, Janet would also take Alice for a ride on Benny, who was apparently very naughty but also particularly kind to both Alice and the boys. When I saw how much Alice loved it, I signed her up to the Riding for the Disabled classes held nearby, with some calm, retired Shetland ponies. Liz, Alice's new nanny in Rutland, would take her to the classes every week, and it was an excellent time for her to ride and be unconditionally cherished. These were brilliantly dreamy days, as well as some of the most unnerving days of my life.

It was Janet who recommended I try potty-training Alice, although I didn't begin this somewhat hilarious experience until after we'd moved to Bath.

To Alice, animals offered something delightful and inexplicable which I'll never be able to adequately describe. Later, when we were in Bath, Pepper, our canine acquisition, showed the same tenderness and love for Alice that the horses did, never complaining when she launched her full, wriggling body weight on top of the unsuspecting Labrador.

9

The Pretty Perfect First Year

Before we left Rutland, way before we had even decided we had to move again, all the children were still young, and life was relatively straightforward. David was away two or three nights a week, either visiting businesses up North or checking in with vital contacts in London. As a baby, Alice was perfect – sweet, gentle and uncomplaining. She was born precisely to term, on her due date. Weirdly, that was also the date David had asked me to marry him seven years previously, in the Rose Garden in Hyde Park.

When she was born, Alice was beautiful to look at, with a winning and ever-ready smile from early on. The excerpt below is from a book I read recently:

> To a parent, your child wasn't just a person: your child was a place, a kind of Narnia, a vast eternal place where the present you were living and the past you remembered and the future you longed for all existed at once. You could see it every time you looked at her: layered in her face was the baby she'd been and the child she'd become and the adult she would grow up to be, and you saw them all simultaneously, like a 3-D image. It made your head spin. It was a place you could take refuge, if you knew how to get in. And each time you left it, each time your child passed out of your sight, you feared you might never be able to return to that place again.
>
> *Little Fires Everywhere* by Celeste Ng

I love this short passage. Celeste Ng describes so eloquently the way I felt about Alice. She was a place where I loved to be, one that, sadly, I was eventually forced to leave.

There were a few things that worried me quite early on in Alice's life, but they were never adequately looked into as they didn't seem like real or recognisable problems. For example, sometimes, from the age of about two weeks, she'd wake in the middle of the night making a gasping sound as if she was frantically struggling to get air. She slept in the bedroom next to ours and, except in times of illness, never slept in our room. This wasn't unusual for us, as none of our children had slept in our room. We had a maternity nurse for each of our children, which had been a generous gift from David's mother, Anne. When I first noticed the gasping sounds at night, Alice's maternity nurse, Judy, was still in situ and was sound asleep in Alice's room. Her loud snoring kept all other sounds at bay, so even she didn't wake up at the sound of Alice's gasps. But somehow, my 'mother's ear' enabled me to hear Alice above the noisy night vibrations. In fact, this sound always woke me – a noise as if she was drowning in air. I'd sit up with a start and hold my breath for a few seconds until she was quiet. I never got to her in time to witness what was happening. Despite running into her bedroom numerous times, I never actually saw any of these episodes.

It was only recently that I remembered when this breathing problem had probably first occurred. Alice was only a few days old and was having her first bath. Judy was bathing her, and as she picked Alice up out of the tub and laid her on the warm towel on the floor beside her, Alice cried out. Both her arms suddenly shot out, almost as if she had just received an unexpected shock, or been stung by a bee. She was gasping so fast and labouring so hard to try to fill her lungs with air, that I genuinely thought she was having what I thought a panic attack might look like. The episode finished as quickly as it started and I'm ashamed to admit that at the time I thought, *Oh no! She's going to be one of those anxious, self-obsessed girls!* She made the same noises that

I would hear later when she woke me up in the next-door bedroom.

How dreadful for me to write this, and to confront, in broad daylight, in clear, black typed letters, how opinionated I was. Just to recap: Alice was a newborn baby, my darling baby girl, who later turned out to be suffering from chronic seizures. A child who never complained, a child I could not have loved or devoted myself to any more than I did. How soberly objectionable that this would be my first thought regarding her seizure, and how shamefully wrong I was.

David and I have recently had whooping cough and the noises of her frantically gasping for air weren't too dissimilar to the gross whoop of our coughs as we tried to suck back the air being involuntarily expelled from our lungs.

Everything pottered on normally for nearly a year after Alice's birth. There was nothing of particular note about her early weeks, except for those strange and unsettling episodes when she woke in the night as if gasping for air. But she always seemed to settle herself afterwards. By now, the episodes had mostly passed. She was never disturbed during the day; I never saw anything that screamed out at me as being unusual or worrying.

Aside from the inexplicable breathing episodes, one of her eyes began to 'diverge', or rather drift off and it would physically move and turn out to look towards something in the direction of her ear. So, she would be looking at me with both her eyes and enjoying whatever was going on in her direct line of vision and then one of her eyes would seemingly get distracted and think that there was something better going on elsewhere! More likely, the muscle/nerves that had been keeping both eyes in tandem had stopped working. As soon as I noticed this, I whisked her off to our GP, who referred Alice to a local paediatric optometrist (children's eye doctor). I was given sweet girly patches with cheerful cartoon designs to put on her good eye to force the other one to focus correctly. This was to try and ensure that her eye would not neurologically 'turn off', thereby eventually making her blind in that eye.

This didn't seem particularly unusual as I'd seen many youngsters with boy-themed patches, or little girls with girly eye patch designs, toddling about at mother and baby groups. I was fairly relaxed about this. All seemed fine until I noticed that it was not always the same eye that was misbehaving. Maybe I should also have taken more notice of a comment made by the optometrist, who said it was unusual for a child to have a divergent squint. If a child has a lazy eye, this usually means that this eye will drift towards to the centre of the face, above the nose. With a divergent squint, we are talking about an eye that looks out towards the ear. Had I looked more carefully into this somewhat unusual development, would things have turned out differently? I doubt that very much; in fact, I can say with confidence that it would, almost certainly, not have made the slightest difference at all to the eventual outcome. However, it might have alerted me to the fact that Alice was beginning to show signs of divergence in other areas, too.

Most concerning was the fact that she began to lose previously attained baby goals. Nearly crawling regressed to not quite bunny-hopping, and the cross-lateral (notice the language that is starting to creep in here) crawling almost began, as did standing. This had started while holding on to the side of the bath, but didn't progress into walking until much later, after hours of physiotherapy and hard work on Alice's part. She used to sit up straight, her muscles having been strengthened in her Bumbo chair, but nothing was moving on and, worse, things seemed to be deteriorating.

Then one day, having woken Alice from her afternoon nap, while I was carrying her downstairs, I felt her head lolling uncomfortably on my shoulder like a newborn's. My stomach lurched, and at that point, I began to think there was definitely something wrong. I called my GP, booked an appointment and, after I saw him with Alice to explain her symptoms and my nagging worries, he swiftly referred me to a paediatrician.

10

The Paediatrician

Alice was a little over one by the time we saw someone about her development. I went to meet the paediatrician at the local hospital, together with David and Alice. He took a few details about what her life had been like so far and did various physical tests on her, one of which consisted of him swinging her up high and then down quickly. This is something I have always referred to, probably incorrectly, as the 'start' test. Would she be happy to be thrust towards the ground, or, worse, dropped? Well, it seemed to be no problem for Alice, she smiled and passively enjoyed the alarming ride. She didn't reach out her hands to protect her head or innately make a move to shield herself. This was a 'skill' that had not crossed my mind as worth testing with her older brothers. I'd never have thought that the instinct to reach out to protect oneself from falling is a life skill, but of course it is. Having never felt the need to experiment by dropping either of my other children to the floor, I didn't have a bank of 'normal reactions' to refer to. It was only when it was pointed out to me by the paediatrician that I realised Alice's lack of reaction was a cause for concern.

The doctor proceeded with the traditional line of questioning: "I'm sorry to have to ask this, but are you and your husband related?"

We both immediately answered, "No!"

The second question – "Does your daughter know her name?" – was met with a little more uncertainty. Possibly I could have called out, 'button' in the correct tone, and Alice would have turned her head to me.

"I'm not sure," I said.

"OK. Does Alice have a favourite toy?"

I could only think that every toy she had was a favourite. "Ummm… I'm not sure…"

I felt this doctor was clutching at the straws suddenly blowing in the violent and noisy winds around our heads. Little did he know that his questions about the things that Alice could or couldn't (mostly couldn't) do were like venomous snakes, poised to attack us and destroy our natural preconceptions about Alice and her future.

In his subsequent report, he concluded that Alice 'still has some difficulty in controlling her head and trunk, cannot sit on her own and does not put out her hands to stop herself from falling sidewards'. She 'is making attempts at reaching out and grabbing toys with immature palmar grasp... she is not transferring yet and has difficulty in getting things to her mouth... She can hold a toy but does not look for a hidden toy'. She 'is making definite developmental progress, but remains delayed without any detected underlying cause'.

Looking at the report now, I can see that at this point, the paediatrician was listing her developmental scales as all roughly the same. She was delayed by about three to four months in every area, speech being probably her worst: 'Alice is babbling, but there is no consistent double syllable babble, and there is no jargon or identifiable words.' Given she was only thirteen months old, and behind by three to four months, it was looking serious.

Despite this tentative diagnosis that Alice was 'delayed' and slower than average, the word 'disabled' was never mentioned, and even when she died, it was not a word that was a part of my vocabulary. I do now use it apologetically on occasion. It's quicker and less complicated to say she was disabled than to try to explain what she was really like. In other words, the fact that Alice looked normal and healthy, and that she did all the things/most of the things/some of the things... that most children do, and yet she was very different from most children in her development, is a difficult thing to 'drop into the conversation'

After we left the hospital, David and I slowly clambered into the car, with our new, hefty, unidentifiable weight wrapped awkwardly around our shoulders. We managed this without uttering a word to each other, carefully placing Alice in her baby seat. The silence crashed dangerously between us, but there was nothing to say. Alice was asleep by then, and we were both lost in our very personal, comfortless thoughts.

When we got home, no one could have known or understood the life-altering bomb that we had just been handed. I remember telling Amanda, Alice's young, inexperienced nanny, the rather vague news about the 'significant and yet unknown delays'. At this time, Amanda had not been working for us for long, and her reaction was typical of someone so young. She burst into tears, and I assumed she was grieving for Alice as well as for me. However, she told me that she was upset because the holiday she had been planning with her boyfriend might have fallen through. This was hard to stomach. While my world had been shaken irrevocably by the prospect of my daughter's delayed development, Alice's nanny was faced with the problem of possibly having to choose a different holiday. But she soon proved to be a sensitive and very loving young woman, one who I'm sure would no longer recognise this behaviour in herself.

I managed to listen to her woes and offer some inadequate "Oh, sorry"s and "Poor you"s, but I knew I had to extricate myself from a potentially dangerous situation before I said something I'd regret. Amanda is still a friend, and maybe this story just illustrates clearly how we are all trapped on our own, sometimes friendless, journeys. I don't judge any one person's voyage as being more or less severe; it is more to do with how we can cope with our own challenges. I could not have survived in any way without the knowledge that Jesus was walking by my side, and sometimes metaphorically carrying me. We all have the choice to react to our suffering, or that of others, in any way we can. My choice was to cling to God.

I left the room and staggered over to the building outside that David used as an office. Without any ceremony, I dropped to my knees on the stony ground and wept. But before I lost it completely, my rational brain kicked in. There was no reason to cry as we had no real understanding of what had been said by the paediatrician. We'd been told that Alice was 'delayed' but, for all we knew, this might not be for very long, and it might not be as bad as I feared. Later, when I returned to the house, I bumped into Ben in the kitchen, and seeing my swollen eyes and tear-stained cheeks, he asked me what was wrong. While at the same time wanting to shield Ben from my anguish, I tried to explain to him what had been said at the hospital, and I began to cry again.

Ben looked at me with genuine bewilderment, and as I babbled on about Alice's potential problems, and the possible outcomes, and the fact that it was probable that she would never walk, he gently interrupted me.

"But, Mummy," he said, with the refreshing, innocent smile of a five-year-old, "she's just Alice."

Ben's words stopped me in my tracks. Those three ingenuous words suddenly made perfect sense and, wondrously, transported me to a quiet and peaceful place. I instantly recalled the assertion I'd heard from God –

This is My child; I carried it on the cross, it's Mine – which illustrated that none of this was a mistake. The words my young son had spoken so eloquently summed up all I needed to know for now. Alice was precisely as she was meant to be.

David took up golf. It was his way of dealing with 'the Alice news'. He was still thoroughly immersed in setting up his business, and spent some of his spare time – when not focused on our boys or me, or devoting himself to little Alice – working on his golf handicap. For his birthday present, which I had given him two days before Alice's first birthday, I bought him some golf lessons. I had played golf with him once, and thought he might appreciate the tuition. Even though his accuracy with the golf ball was pretty good, his technique was more like that of a cricketer whose aim was to step towards the stationary ball to hit a whopping six across the boundary and into the stands.

David's game improved quickly following his lessons, and I could see what a useful distraction golf was for him. It sometimes meant taking therapeutic walks and watching his little white ball fly through the air, occasionally followed by both him and his shot getting lost in the undergrowth and then sometimes found again. His golf pro was also an excellent therapist for him to connect with, and he became a good friend. They talked about techniques and best theories and clubs in the golfing world, which was just what I thought David needed. The time he spent in this new and different world allowed him to mull things over and subconsciously make sense of the other new and scary world he was inhabiting. David could adjust to our news about Alice in his own time and his own way. He was able to assess and assimilate what Alice's future difficulties might mean for us all as a family. He could then do what he does best: make well-orchestrated and thoughtfully constructed plans.

Now David can talk honestly, and even humorously, about his reaction to the news we were given about Alice. But at the time neither of us mentioned the fact that occasionally he used golf as an escape mechanism. We were very conscious of each other's vulnerability. A puff of wind might have blown us over and out of the secure nest of our marriage. We did our silent best to give each other the space we needed to deal with our emotions as rationally and freely as we could.

After the meeting with the paediatrician, I spent the first week avoiding my little girl. I shied away from making eye contact with Alice, but carried on coping with everything physical that I had always done for her. I took care of her immediate practical needs, but held back from any emotional engagement. Whenever possible, I handed Alice over to anyone who was around – my dearest friend, Kay; my housekeeper, Janet; or Amanda. I deliberately avoided my daughter, both physically and emotionally. I wasn't able to allow myself to be seduced by her smell, the softness of her hair, and especially not by her warm, deep and trusting eyes. I had to begin again and wipe clean the now-shattered slate on which I had lovingly chalked the plans for Alice's life. My hopes and dreams for my daughter were now in the balance, and for now, I had to put a wall around my wobbling jelly heart.

I'd had a whole year of 'Alice the First', or 'Alice Phase One'. This was the Alice who had existed in my mind and those of other people; the Alice we'd had before the consultation with the paediatrician, and long before her differences became apparent. This became the juncture at which I experienced what I now think of as the 'first death', which I was only able to properly recognise and talk about once she'd physically died nearly five years later.

The Alice who would grow up, get married, play games with others, perhaps be musical in a way that I hadn't been, was a hope beginning to fade. This was devastating, and it felt like she'd died. My natural dreams for my daughter had been crumpled up and rubbished in the space of one short meeting in one long afternoon.

11

The First Death

I wept and wept. My hopes, plans and dreams for my daughter were gone, and instead I was being forced to enter this completely other world, the world of the disabled, a world we don't usually see in this country as it's all hidden away. Emotionally, mentally and physically, I found it incredibly challenging to adjust to the fact that I was now a part of that world, a world that was utterly alien to me.

As the hours and days passed, it dawned on me that I didn't know my daughter; I mean *really* know her. And that was terrifying. Every time I looked at Alice, I was aware that she was now a different person to me. I was both shocked and ashamed to admit that I had invented my own version of Alice – a version who was now no more. Instead, the little girl who was living in my house was a stranger, a stranger I would now have to embrace and welcome into my wounded heart as a new version of my child. And, although she was alive and breathing, I found myself consumed with a type of grief. It was grief for the child I'd made up. I hadn't allowed myself to notice that Alice was different. I'd paid no heed to Sheena's comments when she'd suggested that Alice might be delayed. I'd paid no attention when she'd suggested that there was perhaps a problem that I should investigate. Prickly comments, even from a dear friend, that no mum wants to hear, let alone address.

Typically, when you learn something new, you are at least aware of what you're dealing with. For example, when you learn another language, you think, *Well, I know about a country called Spain. I know what Spanish is. It's a foreign language; it's a language they speak in Spain, as well as many other countries, but with different accents!* You also have the tools that enable you to learn another language. So you can, in fact, learn Spanish. Whereas how do you learn about a child with 'developmental delays', who doesn't even have a diagnosis?

After a week of shock and grieving, a week that I had deliberately set aside to hide away emotionally from this stranger I now had living in my house, I began to open my eyes and my battered heart to a brand-new girl. I decided that I wanted to introduce myself to the real Alice. I took off my blinkers and looked at my daughter with virgin eyes that were now wide open and fully accepting. This felt like a rebirth, and one for which I was now ready. I set about finding out about a multitude of things that had been, hitherto, inconveniently hidden from my sight: doctors, diagnoses, prognoses, tests, immediate necessities, future necessities and medical specialists.

I tapped into the world of the National Health Service, but it wasn't enough. I found it impossible to survive living in limbo between what seemed like very occasional appointments. I decided to roam the now-invaluable internet for private physios, speech therapists and occupational therapists, doing all of this with little money of our own. Some of the '–ists' came to us and the others we visited. In and out of our house, I trailed with Alice at my tail, or, more accurately, pushing her ahead of me in her pushchair. I quickly became immersed in a world of specialists: paediatric specialists, physiotherapists, speech and language therapists, occupational therapists, medical specialists, nutritional therapists, music therapists. Wherever there was a therapist or a specialist, there was I, the novice, searching for help, searching for an answer, looking for a cure.

Our weeks became divided up into neat parcels of treatments and visits to specialists. But no amount of therapy was enough. There wasn't enough time for me to catch up on my perceived wasted year of Alice's development. I hired private therapists of three main kinds, two of whom particularly stood out: the physiotherapist,

Sarah, and the occupational therapist, Jane. The only reason the speech and language therapist, Caroline, didn't have similar success was because Alice wasn't able to copy a sound, let alone form anything like a recognisable word herself. Actually, she couldn't even blow or shape her mouth to demand or to mimic someone in front of her. Most of her sounds were wordless squeals and whoops of delight and excitement.

12

South Africa

We'd decided earlier that year, 2007, long before I was on a hunt for the elusive healing genie, that we wanted to spend Christmas in South Africa. Alice would be fifteen months old, Ben would be six and Matthew four. By the time Christmas arrived, I thought I understood Alice; she had been 'diagnosed' at twelve months and I had had three months of getting to know the 'new' her. I was learning to appreciate and love her while hiding my deep fears within a neatly packaged personal space called a 'no-go zone'. I thought I knew her well. I knew her better than anyone; of course I did. I was her mother. I spent most of my time with her. I thought I knew what she was thinking; I thought I knew what she wanted. However, when we were in Cape Town, I realised how horribly deluded I'd been.

We'd taken the long flight from Heathrow, and I'd hired a supposedly specialist chair for Alice to help her to sit upright on the plane. This was an emotional time for me. Things were becoming increasingly hard for Alice, and I found it very challenging to acknowledge the problems we were facing.

During the flight, I don't remember feeding Alice or giving her anything to drink at all. I was too busy lifting or repositioning her, shunting her up again and again as she slipped and slumped down in her questionably unique travel seat. I was busy carrying her to the toilet to change her smelly and wet nappy. Possibly I was preoccupied with thinking about the film I wasn't watching, or the sleep I craved and wasn't getting, or genuinely feeling jealous that my husband was sitting in between the 'normal' boys and enjoying a 'normal' flight. I felt left out of the fun the boys were having with their father in their cosy little group, enjoying the in-flight film, totally oblivious to my distress. I was, possibly for the first time, experiencing the gross differences and loneliness I was going to have to get used to, having a disabled child.

Having left cold and grey England, we arrived in the heat and scorching bright sunshine of the South African summer. We immediately changed into our colourful summer clothes, and all of us donned our sunglasses, which we had excitedly packed in our hand luggage. When we got to our rented house, Ben and Matthew screamed with delight at the sight of the swimming pool and everything about our exquisite temporary home, which stood below the breathtaking Table Mountain in Cape Town. The atmosphere was one of celebration and anticipation. We were expecting my cousin, Charlie, his wife, Sheena, and their two girls, to join us from Zambia – again, more elation. What with the heat, the beauty and the exhilaration of where we were, my mind was a million miles from where it should have been. I was thinking of Alice as a child who was like her brothers, someone who'd speak up for herself, or at least make it known to me what she wanted. However, she'd been quiet since we'd arrived, alternating between smiling and sleeping. She was no longer being breastfed, and possibly (dare I say probably?) I had not given her much food or drink on the plane as there was nothing on offer that would suit her. Typically, I was in the habit of defrosting and heating up little portions of baby food from ice-cube trays, which I hadn't taken with me. But here we were, being swept up and carried off, in anticipation of an exotic family holiday.

Our holiday house was perfect, with a generous terrace spanning the whole of the first floor with views over the glistening Atlantic Ocean. We would watch the sun setting over the water if we were lucky enough to catch it. I'd try to time it so that the boys could watch, but no sooner had I called them and they dashed upstairs, than the sun would dramatically disappear. The sun didn't follow the same attitude as some of the African culture of *polepole* ('slowly-slowly'); it sank as fast as fast-fast could be; as if it was in a race to fall below the horizon before the boys had the chance to race up the stairs and see its fiery beauty.

The pool was below the room Ben and Matthew shared, luckily far enough away and high enough that there was no temptation for them to jump in to cool off. Had the boys been tempted to jump into the cool and invigorating water from a height, there was also the balcony railing to negotiate. Alice's room was next to ours at the top of a glass spiral staircase. To get to the terrace, I could walk the width of our bedroom and open the double doors to see the view, sit on a sun lounger and drink the glass of chilled white wine that David invariably had waiting for me. On the other side of the room was a partial view of the top of Table Mountain. The curtains to this window were electronic, and in the morning, we could sleepily switch the button to open them and reveal the dramatic beauty outside.

It was a heady, delicious time with Charlie and Sheena and their dazzling girls. Their eldest, Shanti, is two years older than Ben, and Salome the same age as him. Sheena and I had been pregnant together and had given birth within three weeks of each other – her last and my first. The girls were, and still are, utterly gorgeous in every way. They'd been brought up in Africa and were inhabitants of the life we were only beginning to experience and subsequently grew to adore. The house was full of children's laughter and happiness, fresh fruit and cold drinks, and an occasional glass of wine with delicious seafood smoking on the braai.

It was sometime during the early afternoon after we'd arrived that I began to notice something was wrong. No doubt many people reading this will have experienced the same forgetfulness that I did on the plane. Maybe Alice just wasn't noisy enough. She was a little, voiceless someone; a girl, I was beginning to realise, we needed to watch.

Not long after we'd arrived at the house, I noticed Alice was becoming more and more tired and listless, and I asked David if we should take her to see a doctor. I began to think there was something wrong with her, perhaps a dangerous bug that she'd caught on the plane, or a cold or a virus that she'd carried with her. Then I thought some more, and at last I awoke from my absurd reverie. I thought about her and not me, and, with a metaphorical slap in the face, I suddenly realised how little she'd been drinking.

I knew how much water I was consuming, how much I required hydration. Now I suddenly realised what a superbly needy child Alice was. A child who needed me. I remember saying to David that I couldn't remember having fed her yet, or having given her anything to drink. I asked him how much he thought he might have given her. I remember suddenly realising that, because Alice hadn't asked for anything, it hadn't occurred to either of us that she might be thirsty. We just hadn't thought; we were in an unfamiliar environment with none of the typical prompts to drink, eat or properly think of anything that a voiceless child might need. Whether I had always been this selfish I shall probably never know, but suddenly I realised, with a shot of ice-cold reality, that I was going to have to learn what it entailed to be properly needed, to be utterly depended upon by my daughter. As soon as I gave Alice a drink and some fruit to eat, she perked up, and she was back to her normal self.

I thought I recognised at the time how things would have to be in the future. I had to be Alice's thoughts, her voice. In fact, I was going to have to become like her, think like her, experience hunger and thirst for her and make sure I was aware of all the needs that she was unable to express, voice or think for herself.

A truly beautiful but also genuinely terrifying responsibility.

David's cousin met up with us in Cape Town. David's father had mentioned that Chris, his wife, Adelle, and their three children were also in South Africa, and coincidentally in the same area as us. It turned out that they just happened to be renting a house in the road behind ours.

Although David knew his cousin, he'd never spent much time with him, but soon after Chris arrived at our house both he and David slipped effortlessly into behaving like long-lost twins. They look similar, and possess the same charm and humour. Adelle has become a really good friend of mine, and their three children are captivating and enchanting in equal measure. Accompanied by my cousin and his family, and now David's cousin with his gang, our holiday was becoming more and more exquisite.

All four adults immediately loved our daughter as if she were their own. Not only that; their four girls seemed to have adopted her into their team. This acceptance and closeness meant more to us than I can adequately convey. A few years later, Adelle walked miles with Alice on the Cornish beaches, guided by the breaking waves on the sand. This time together in South Africa turned out to be the beginning of a welcome and natural friendship for all of us.

The holiday in Cape Town was an enormous success, except for the one thing that was troubling me – the realisation that my life was now thoroughly different, and would continue to be so. I was responsible for a disabled child. As much as I adore our two boys, I knew that one day I would have to let them go willingly. I knew that they'd become independent adults. But this burden of responsibility for Alice would stay with David and me for the rest of her life, as well as for the rest of ours. I realised that, whether I wanted to or not, I'd have to give up so much of my own life as well as some of the time I spent caring for my sons, in order to protect and look after Alice until the day that I either became incompetent, or was six feet under. At this point we had no idea of the severity of her disability and we never suspected that she would not reach adulthood.

Right up until the week before we knew she would die, we were still trying to work out how we would be best able to support the boys in their role as her brothers. David in particular was planning for her future and security once we were gone.

Once we came back to England after our unforgettable holiday, I started hunting in earnest for all we might need for Alice. Quite soon, I found a spectacular physiotherapist.

13

The Physiotherapist

Sarah, Alice's physiotherapist in Rutland, was an unexpected godsend. Between the ages of one-and-a-half and nearly three, she was Alice's friendly carer, torturer and assailant in equal measure. After assessing Alice and then developing a sensible and workable protocol for her, Sarah showed me how to fit Alice's legs into gaiters! These seemed archaic and, worse, tortuous; they weren't, but they looked like they could be.

Amazing, marvellous, cheerful and gentle Sarah applied tools that appeared to do nothing except tear my heart out of my chest. She sensitively explained her techniques to me, showing me the benefits of learning how to exercise sitting in an upright position with straight legs lying ahead of you. These are proven exercises for those who cannot access their muscles in the usual fashion.

To make it clear to me why Alice would benefit from the exercises, Sarah asked me to perform some of them for myself. Once I'd had first-hand experience, I realised how utterly exhausting they were. I obviously didn't have gaitors to use, but I did a version of the exercise that gave me enough information to realise that these were very powerful.

We started by strapping the gaiters onto her legs. The idea was to lift one of Alice's legs first and place it a few degrees away from the other, and then lift the second leg and join it up with its partner. I watched passively as my precious daughter was strapped into these hard plastic 'leggings' that ran from her hips to her ankles. I then helped her to move her legs around an imaginary clock while I accompanied her movements with songs like 'The Wheels on the Bus' and 'Hickory Dickory Dock'. I swallowed hard and forced myself to hold back the tears.

Only Sarah kept me sane. I never wanted her to leave; I wanted to drink in her knowledge and to be continually clothed in her kindness. Sometimes I felt I was going mad, but Sarah's knowledge and professionalism consoled me. Painstakingly, I lifted Alice's legs, one after the other, to help her gain a modicum of core strength. Over the weeks, months and years, I moved her again and again round the imaginary musical clock, not knowing that this same clock was also counting down her days with us. I'd smile at her, all the while feeling like a crazy woman. I'd sing and giggle nursery rhymes over and over as I lifted her legs and moved her round and round, and then round and round again. She smiled on passively, trusting me.

From the gracious expression on her face, Alice seemed to take for granted the fact that I loved her and that this was a good thing to be doing. Intellectually I knew that these dreadful exercises were meant to help, but it was hard. The worst thing was that we – and by that I mean the physiotherapist and I – didn't know for certain whether this would eventually do any good.

Although there was never any guarantee that this would prove effective, never any assurance that it would do anything other than waste my breath and break my heart, I carried on. I never stopped singing and lifting her legs in the hope that one day this would be over and Alice would suddenly get up and walk.

Then one day, about three years later, that is exactly what she did.

How absurd it sounds that I thought I'd find a cure and make Alice 'whole'. At the time, this treatment was made even more distressing for me, as I could see how pathetically weak Alice was and how hard it was for her to move her legs from side to side. Despite taking part in everything that was being done to help Alice, I still felt like a passive onlooker placing all my hopes in those who had more knowledge than I. It was undoubtedly thanks to Sarah's diligence, kindness and courage, as well as her own determination, that Alice did eventually walk. The ability to be self-propelling made Alice phenomenally happy and the rest of us inordinately proud.

Sarah was always delighted with Alice's attitude and flexibility. "Well done, Alice. Well done! Very good!" she'd proclaim. I found it hard to accept that this minute amount of progress was perceived as 'good' by Sarah. I had to set my face into this new and bitter wind and hope that Alice's demanding exercises wouldn't be in vain. I had to hope that I would find more of the right people who could give me the keys to her lonely jail.

Even though at this time, Alice wasn't able to walk at all, we spent a lot of time 'patterning' it for her, so that she would learn what it was meant to feel like. Following Sarah's meticulous instructions, I would position my forearm and hand under Alice's lower arm and hand and start to walk with Alice leaning on me for support, while Sarah did the same on her other side. Then Sarah would take Alice's lower leg and physically move the leg forward. She would plant it on the ground in a forward position to show Alice what it would feel like to propel herself forward.

At the beginning, this always had to be done by the two of us. Sarah and I would discreetly giggle as we tried to perfect this movement. It felt a little bit like we were choreographing something as involved as a Torvill and Dean bolero routine, hopefully without ending up being thrown onto the floor! I enjoyed our time together as we struggled to teach Alice the invaluable skill of walking. This was physically demanding as we bent over and stumbled slowly forwards while trying not to get in the way of each other or Alice. If it was tiring for us, it must have been so much harder for my little girl. I found it extremely challenging as her mother, wanting to protect and comfort her, yet also knowing that I had to push and demand things of her. There was also no guarantee that these hours and hours of physical exhaustion, or my well of hope, would ever materialise into anything.

Even though Alice learnt to do things physically, she struggled mentally to understand the process. She wasn't yet steady enough on her feet to be led by just one person, and I honestly didn't expect that she would ever be able to walk by herself. She had tried to walk with a walking frame, but it was too complicated. This involved holding on to the frame, whilst moving one leg at a time forwards and transferring her weight from one leg to another in order to walk. It was far too complex a movement and too much to ask of her at this stage.

Months after these early introductions to the ambulation experience, Alice did manage to walk, moving her legs and feet unaided, but still with Sarah and me either side of her. Eventually, we were able to progress to just one person holding her lower arm and hand, and then a year or so later, one person kept hold of her hand. All of this was so painstakingly slow it was hard to see the changes in her. I only had a session with Sarah once a month, and in the meantime I was in charge of continuing the exercise with Amanda, or alone as best I could. I found that often I was concentrating on her lack of progress rather than appreciating the small amount of success Alice did achieve.

14

More Therapists

I also employed a speech and language therapist, another dedicated, very proficient woman who presented immaculately and lived in a house renovated in like manner within a mile or two of our home. Not only was she smartly dressed, but she was also incredibly professional. She had never worked with a child with Alice's mysterious difficulties before and had to be imaginative in her style and adapt her methods to suit a little girl who couldn't even blow, never mind mimic sounds.

Shortly before Alice died, I once lifted her out of her hospital bed, and, as I carried her in my arms, she managed a very distinctive "Mama". I can't speak about this, even now, without my eyes welling up with pride married with grief. Was this simply an exhalation of air from her lungs, or did she say the word intentionally? I want to think she meant to say it as a gift to me. The same week, when we were in Bristol Children's Hospital, David was holding Alice, and she was repeatedly banging her cheek against his. Eventually, she managed to kiss his cheek with her lips. I was so glad I was there to watch this and to be able to tell David, as he'd been too close to see what she'd been trying so hard to do. Again, I have to believe this was a deliberate, meaningful action on Alice's part, and not an overenthusiastic imagining on mine.

Meanwhile, in the early days, I made all the doctors' appointments, specialist appointments, any bloody appointment, while we explored the eternal question: what was wrong with Alice?

In the end, though, it turned out my son was right.

She was just Alice.

The other intense therapy I found for Alice was through an occupational therapist. Jane was another woman who played a pivotal role in our lives. She was Alice's first, and all-time best, occupational therapist. If you had asked me before I had Alice, I might have assumed an occupational therapist was someone who looked after people who had occupations they didn't like and needed counselling for it! Funny.

Jane was the most forward-thinking and devoted occupational therapist I have ever had the privilege of meeting. In those early days, I had no idea how much I would depend on her, nor how much she would give both me and Alice. If other people in our lives were sometimes pure gold, Jane was pure gold with bells, bubbles, whistles, trampolines, climbing frames, music and laughter on top. When we subsequently moved to Bath, I was expecting to find like-minded, equally well-trained and experienced professionals, but no one came anywhere near her shining brilliance, let alone her sensitivity and kindness.

Jane's treatment room was filled with tunnel games, swings of every description, slides, bubbles, musical sounds and moving objects. Her magnificent treasure trove was second to none. Matthew came along one day to see what all the fuss was all about, and he loved it. A child's playroom with bright colours and moving objects to sit on and be flung over.

Alice was thrown about and swung around and spun around and tumbled about. She smiled from ear to ear while I looked on, desperately hoping to see some change or awakening in her. After a session, she would collapse into an exhausted, peaceful and happy sleep. Jane was the first professional who spotted a quiet determination in Alice. I was concentrating on all the things Alice was lacking and those she was failing in, it took me another three years to genuinely see what Jane could so clearly see from early on. She spotted a resolution in Alice that many of us, and certainly I, were too blind to see.

Most of Jane's work was with children on the autistic spectrum, so there were very few, if any, with Alice's complex needs. Jane was nevertheless delighted to try anything and experiment with different things. I was a keen onlooker, hoping, always hoping, that something would be unlocked in Alice that would prove pivotal to her development. It's difficult to write this because in retrospect I can see how futile all of this was and how frankly irrelevant. Perhaps if she were still alive, then I would paint a different picture. I might even be clinging on to the next meeting, the next treatment, the next hope that an expert might be able to help and give us a brighter, easier future for our daughter.

Although at the time I had become an expert in all things Alice, my proficiency never extended to an interest in caring for other children with similar difficulties. Even today, I cannot bring myself to spend time with children who need the most help. I have good reason now; it's just too desperately sad for me. I see Alice in every one of those children, and I want to melt into a heap of grief because she is no longer here. After reading *Eye Can Write* by Jonathan Bryan, I can see how children with difficulties bring out the best possible and unconditional love in me, but because of what happened to our family it remains emotionally impossible for me to interact with them.

Perhaps I use the pain of having lost Alice to protect me from exposure to those most in need. The door to Alice's world, which opened for us so suddenly, shut just as quickly the day she died. I had become very good at spotting gifted carers and an expert at seeing love in others; perhaps when enough time has passed, I might be able to bend down and serve those who are most deserving. I hope so.

From the age of one through to her second year, I knew that Alice was a disabled child. I knew it as a fact, but during all this time I was still stumbling along with my eyes elsewhere on a road that might hopefully be kinder to her. The knowledge that she was disabled was like a mist of a new reality hovering over me. I didn't think of it as a permanent thing, but rather as something that would miraculously lift with a warm sun, like the light fog that disappears on a hazy English summer's day. Maybe because she'd never been referred to as disabled by anyone in the medical profession, I found it hard to come to terms with the stark reality of our situation. The fact that I'd never heard anyone use the 'D' word about Alice during her lifetime made it seem almost as if it had become a swear word or, worse, a derogatory term. However, when we were told that Alice had 'learning difficulties' I wanted to explain that they were a little more than 'difficulties'. They were more like learning impossibilities.

She was a severely disabled child, and where is the shame in that?

Her brother's profound statement – "Mum, she's just Alice" – kept me sane in the heat of many of the testing moments and demanding days with our little girl.

During the first year since 'discovering' my new child, she and I explored a different world together. We played with plasticine and fiddled with various toys that spun round and round. Plastic shapes filled her world, and she chose what interested her, or rather, I decided what I thought should interest her, as she never made any obvious choices herself.

The harder I pushed Alice, the more she loved it. I was given a mini chair by the NHS, with a removable tabletop and a fitted seat where she spent many hours. I would run around, scooping up items that might grab her attention. I hoped for something that would unlock her slow, almost imperceptible changes. I crouched on the ground and handed the objects to her. Dried pasta shapes, mini Disney figures, Lego characters purloined from the boys. Like me, she loved anything that was a surprise; anything musical. Toys that played second-rate echoes of famous tunes. More often than not, she'd let these toys drop to the floor when she'd had enough of them or her muscles had fatigued. She never dropped them deliberately, though I'd have been happy if she had, since we were still trying to teach her to put things down or let things go purposely.

Another thing Alice loved was water. She adored the sensation of it around her body and the freedom of movement it gave her. If it was freezing cold, it didn't matter to Alice as she kicked and splashed and stretched her way hopefully towards my dream for her independence. She sat in a toddler's water chair, floating, grinning and 'laughing', in the various pools we visited. When she was in the water, I can only imagine she must have had a rare feeling of being unrestrained by a body that was so cumbersome, uncooperative and downright disobedient.

Unfortunately, she loved swimming regardless of not only the temperature of the water, but the weather outside as well. I drew the line at jumping into an unheated pool with a cold and blustery wind as a swimming costume in order to entertain her while on our Cornish holidays. I do, however, have plenty of photographic evidence of the other willing martyrs in and outside the family who chose to join Alice in her watery games. In the pool, Alice's face was radiant, with a smile that melted the ice on the surface, as well as warming the soul of her bathing companion. Naomi, who was the daughter of the boys' headmaster, babysat for us occasionally when we were in Bath. She took on the responsibility that came with caring for Alice and shared in some of the good times as well as the excruciating end. I grew to love her very deeply. Naomi always got on with the job in hand and did everything with Alice – often things that I didn't dare to do, such as volunteer to go into the swimming pool when it was almost cold enough to see the breath from your mouth. Nothing was too much for Naomi, and she loved Alice with a rare quality which I'll never forget and could never undervalue.

It's hard for me to remember the pain I experienced daily. The sorrow for both Alice and myself, although obviously in her case it was more my perception of her anguish, which I don't think she truly experienced until she was very ill in the last six months of her life. For me, it was the pain and lonely sorrow of knowing that my years were evermore to be spent leaving my marriage on the dustheap of neglect. I was getting used to the sadness of being left alone with my daughter while David took care of our sons. Even writing this now, so long after she went, I feel the nudge and knock of the 'I' and 'me', terms which primarily look after the self. I imagined we would have Alice for the whole of our lives, I had no reason to think otherwise. I am richer for having been stretched out of my comfort zone, and I am now so much poorer for having lost her and everything she demanded of me.

The holiday cottages we rented in Cornwall were ideal for the boys, but not always for a disabled child. There might be awkward steps down to the beach, or a long walk along the sand with Alice in her pushchair, usually with an accompanying biting wind lashing our faces. Invariably the sand clogged the wheels of the pushchair while our cold ears burnt with pain. And sometimes this was during the summer months!

Alice was never miserable in the cold. She loved anything that gave her enhanced proprioceptive information. 'Proprioceptive' was another new word for me, meaning the position-movement sensation which offers a heightened level of physiologic information. The actual meaning of 'proprioception' is when a physical movement becomes so apparent that your brain says, *Ah, so that's what I'm doing!* 'Proprioceptive enhancement' means that you are helped to gain a sense of awareness of physical movement. Any external stimulation is a form of proprioceptive knowledge.

This position-movement sensation was described initially in 1557 by Julius Caesar Scaliger as a 'sense of locomotion'. Much later in 1826, Charles Bell expounded the idea of a 'muscle sense', which is credited as one of the first descriptions of physiologic feedback mechanisms. Bell's view was that commands are carried from the brain to the muscles, and that reports on the muscles' condition are then sent in the reverse direction as you see the beneficial new information that you are gathering. 'Muscle memory' is perhaps a more succinct description of this process.

Life could be messy with Alice around. I didn't help matters by buying a large, flat, black plastic tray similar to a sandpit with a smaller lip. This became Alice's paint pool, which meant investing in lots of kid-friendly, primary-colour paints in large tubes which we then squirted in snail-like lumps onto the tray. Clothed only in her nappy, Alice would sit inside this tray, surrounded by colourful sludges of bright paint. She'd grin wildly, shrieking with joy while making lots of mess, the blobs smeared all over her tummy as well as the base of the tray. Later we would wipe this clean, before sponging off all the colours that were plastered all over Alice. Since she smeared paint over her face and in her hair, we had to be careful that as little as possible reached her mouth. She loved to play freely in this sticky mess, but on the whole, all it proved to do was elicit roars of laughter from anyone who saw us. I mostly left this colourful job to our home help, Amanda and after her came Liz, who had taken over from Amanda when she moved on. Liz would work with Alice while I schooled the boys. Teaching them was relatively calm and, most of the time, less noisy and messy than looking after Alice, and almost certainly less entertaining!

We created fun for Alice, and she, in turn, created more for herself, as well as for us. The fact that her life was in some ways so chaotic challenged me deeply. I found it very hard. Losing control scared me on some, or should I say all, levels. Gradually our house was filling with physio equipment and sensory tools and iPads and books. Books that I read to learn more, and children's books that we read to Alice and the boys. Fictional tales that painted our world, and real tales that smudged or sometimes brightened it. Our home was always going to be identifiable as the home of a disabled child, and, despite my aversion to chaos, I was secretly proud of this accolade. All the accessories that filled our world were proof of our diligence and devotion to our daughter. The more mess and disruption there was around us, the more it felt like Alice must be learning and growing. I wanted our home to be her home. I wanted it to be like her own garden in which she could grow, improve, and life could be easier.

I tried many other things to help Alice learn; things that I hoped might ignite her innate ability to do so. I'm conscious of the fact that I have used the word 'innate'; of course, if anything had been innate, then there would have been no need for me to have ignited anything. But Alice had very little of this intrinsic programming, and this was the stumbling block. Her blueprint was faulty and lacking in most essential things. Do I sound negative? Maybe this is why it's taken me so long to write sincerely about Alice. Possibly, by writing honestly now, I'm having to face the hard truths instead of pretending they didn't exist.

One of the things I did to try to make decision-making interesting for Alice was to present her with choices. I painted four A4-sized MDF boards in a neutral colour and then stuck on long strips of Velcro so that I could attach different pictures to them. For example, she could choose a snack from the 'Snack' board, on which I had attached images of food options for her – maybe a banana, or strawberry yoghurt, or a packet of raisins. There was also a 'Drink' board with an image of a glass of water, or a carton of Ribena with a straw. Another option might be 'Playtime', with a photo of her on the swing, or playing on the trampoline with her brothers, or with a musical toy. There were endless options for us to thumb through and to entertain us.

I put these images and many more onto cards, which I then laminated, for the different choices we could make. I could then pick through the options and Velcro these onto the relevant boards. The idea was that Alice could look at them and point to one, if not with her finger, then with her eyes, thus helping with decision-making, and her eventual autonomy. Truthfully, it was me who made the choices as she was never able to point either with her finger or by moving her eyes. At least it meant, once I had decided what we were going to do, I could show her the card, verbalise the choice and then let her know what was coming up next. I made similar boards for other daily events, but I still hadn't found anything which could set her off, off and away to the land of self-discovery.

Around the same time, I introduced small laminated images that I attached to my wrist. I had been given an elasticated wristband that could hold ten or more images. The idea was that Alice could pull and grab one to show me what she wanted. Unfortunately, this was never useful apart from occupying me in many enjoyable hours as I chose, printed, cut and then laminated pictures from magazines, Google or my personal photos. I then carefully attached these to the wristband. Alice never appeared to choose, she probably never minded, and she never complained. Everything seemed to be a pleasure to her.

Only those who have spent time with very young children know the utter dependence that a child who is between birth and approximately nine months old has on the adults around them. Alice was between one and three years old when I was introducing these schemes. In mental capacity, however, she could still be judged as being about nine months old. Alice had the complete dependence of a baby, and she had trust in bucket loads.

Meanwhile, neither we nor the specialists were any nearer to finding an explanation for Alice's difficulties. We had no understanding of what was wrong with our little girl or, even more importantly, how we could make her better. She looked so 'normal'; it seemed very strange that Alice wasn't able to communicate like other children of her age did, especially as, when she caught our eye and held our gaze, she seemed to be one hundred per cent present. I'm convinced she was listening and taking things in.

I remember saying to David one day, that when you were with Alice, it was like having a tape recorder recording everything. It seemed that she was taping everything that was said to her; the only thing she didn't have was the ability to respond and play the tape back. Although change was hard to see, once, at about this time, my father-in-law, Anthony, with his consistently limitless hoard of optimism, famously said, "All Alice has to do now is learn to speak!"

I spent the next few years trying to change Alice. Looking back, I wonder why I did this, and also question my trust in God. I don't feel guilty or bad about the exercises and the teaching programmes I put Alice through. I just think that it might have all been an unnecessary waste of time and energy. But throwing myself into these programmes, hooking up with all the therapists – these things, these people, all of these activities – kept me from going completely mad. And I can't deny that the teaching programmes eventually enabled Alice to walk, and us all to experience and share in the feelings of achievement and freedom that walking ultimately gave her.

I was still preoccupied with looking for an explanation

as to why she was delayed, looking for a magical 'cure'. All this while, David was indefatigably setting up his business. We were hunting for the elusive magic pot of gold with which to pay for the crippling expenses we were experiencing as a family with a disabled child.

15

America

Before we were thrown onto the epileptic roundabout, when Alice was a little over one-and-a-half, Sophie, David's sister, who was now living in North Carolina, suggested that we visit a university hospital in the States which had a department specialising in rare genetic diseases. The team at University of North Carolina (UNC) Medical Centre in Chapel Hill proved to be tremendously understanding and willing to explore everything. Sadly, in the end, and through no fault of their own, they proved to be impressively unproductive.

We took the plane from Heathrow to North Carolina and drove to stay at Sophie's house. She had moved there with her family about three years previously. Unusually, they were not there, and it was a shame that the house was empty, but their absence did mean that we could concentrate on Alice and everything that the medics were doing without any distraction, however welcome.

From the first time we walked through the electric doors at the hospital, we felt confident that we were dealing with an organisation that knew what they were doing. We were seen at the appointed time with no delays, and from the very beginning, we met up with the whole disciplinary team. This included the three areas I had already been concentrating on: occupational therapy, physiotherapy, and speech and language therapy. I didn't feel I had to spoon-feed these highly efficient professionals, and what was unusual, based on my experience to date, was that they were all working in tandem with each other. They were speaking to each other and bouncing ideas off one another. At the time, I was only beginning to understand the value of these disciplines, so this was reassuring. I felt sure they'd be able to figure out the Alice conundrum. They observed and then wrote their assessments, spoke to each other and wrote down their conclusions, and then talked again to make sure that they had not missed anything. I was utterly blown away. I genuinely felt that we would certainly get to the bottom of 'the problem with Alice' and everything would be fixed. After this, we would move into the land of 'done', 'mended' and totally 'normal'.

This took an enormous amount of pressure off my shoulders. I didn't have to keep trying to remember what had been said, by whom and to what import. We met up with the doctors, the neurologist, the haematologist, the paediatrician. They seemed to know exactly what they were doing, and how it fitted in with each colleague's goals. Their confidence was infectious, and for those few short days, I felt hopeful and at peace.

On our second day there, the medical team explained that they were going to give Alice a general anaesthetic and then run all the medical tests. They'd be taking her blood and afterwards dividing the samples up for the different doctors who were all experts in their own disciplines. Only then could the detailed exploration begin, and, following that, an assessment and conclusion would be passed round to everybody. They would also be doing an in-depth brain scan and comparing it with the one that we'd already had done in England. They would then get together with the multidisciplinary team to discuss their findings, which in turn would give us the means to move forward. I think they fully expected to come back to us with concrete answers and possible solutions.

I was excited that the end was in sight and I would be given my daughter back whole, possibly even cured, or if not that, then at least on the road to a change for the better. In one week, we managed to do what I'd spent months trying to do at home in England.

We left Alice at the hospital, having been there with her when they gave her the drugs to send her to sleep. I was very emotional as I said goodnight to her when she was given the general anaesthetic and lost consciousness. I must admit I felt terrified at the thought of Alice going under a general anaesthetic and having no contact with her for a few hours. Supposing she had an adverse reaction to the drugs? For the first time in her life, everything was out of my control.

Needless to say, no answers were forthcoming from the scan, except that her missing corpus callosum was confirmed, which is the bridge of nervous tissue that connects the two sides of the brain and allows communication between them. When we had this result in the UK, one report on this finding said that it was not a significant matter, and another said the opposite! What to believe?! It's so ironic writing this now, knowing what we had to face later on in her short life. I believe with all my heart that God sees everything from the beginning to the end. I'm glad I could experience that day in North Carolina as simply 'that day in North Carolina'. I'm comforted that I had no view of any of the other days we were going to have to go through in the not-too-distant future.

While Alice was in the hospital, David and I wandered around the outskirts of the grounds. I suppose we didn't talk much about anything as our minds were elsewhere. David pushed the empty pushchair in front of him, and we could only think of our missing child and where she was and whether or not anything meaningful would be discovered following the investigations.

We were half-heartedly looking for somewhere to find a coffee and a snack when a young, athletic-looking American man passed us on his morning jog. As he caught sight of the empty pushchair, he paused and, without warning, his face lit up. In a thick American drawl, he quipped, "Looks like you've lost someone!"

In most situations this might have been funny; however, when we informed him that our daughter was under a general anaesthetic in the hospital, he was genuinely apologetic, and jogged on. He meant no harm and, of course, neither he nor we had any idea that one day, our metaphorical pushchair would remain empty forever.

16

Peroxisomal Disorder

There was a point when David and I thought we'd found out what was 'wrong with Alice'. We were back from the States, living in Rutland, and I took my usual trip to London in my continual quest for the latest, greatest, most illuminating medical tests. The tests had come back blank from the States, and we'd had many, many investigations in the UK, which had also drawn blanks. However, the professionals at the Portland Hospital, and then those at Great Ormond Street Hospital, thought they'd found something, and it was not a nice something.

It started when David and I took Alice to London to see a paediatrician specialising in optometry at the Portland Hospital. Those three little words in a neat sentence, 'went to London', give no accurate indication of the massive amount of preparation involved in taking that trip with a young, disabled child. Food had been carefully bought, puréed and then frozen, subsequently to be defrosted and warmed through, stirred and put in an appropriate travel-sized container. I also had to make sure Alice had a drink; I usually gave her water in an appropriate sippy cup that she could drink from without spilling liquid everywhere. She also needed a change of clothes, which was usually a fresh pair of trousers and sometimes a T-shirt, depending on how dribbly she was. I eventually bought fabric bibs for her to wear all the time because her salivating could become so profuse. We also needed the typical plastic feeding bibs for the unavoidable mess from lunch, snacks or water.

Alice was also likely to produce a sizeable wet poo that would inevitably spill out of her nappy and over the top of her trousers. Then, of course, I needed plastic bags. One for the clean change of clothes, and one for the likely smelly ones that had just been removed. Another for the tubs that held the baby food, and possibly one to contain the 'stuff' we didn't want to touch the 'other stuff' in the bag.

Then there were the toys. Fiddle toys, chew toys, comforting toys and musical toys. As I write this, I realise that these were probably toys that interested me more than Alice; toys that I hoped would awaken in her an ability to react and interact more traditionally.

I hope I never made her feel that she wasn't enough, or that she needed to change. I just wanted her to develop in a way that would mean that I could understand her more clearly without the constant pressure and responsibility of being her assumed voice and thoughts. I was beginning to long for a time when I wouldn't be the only port of call for her, or for others wanting to know more about her. The strange thing about writing this, now that our boys are teenagers, is that I long for the ability to make decisions for them and to be their port of call and their director. I actually want to be the one to make the decisions that I feel are in their best interest. And yet there I was in just this position with Alice, and complaining. The ludicrous irony!

We had an appointment with the paediatric neurologist specialising in optometry at the Portland Hospital, whom we'd travelled a hundred miles to see, and I spent seemingly thousands of hours preparing for. We arrived at the hospital, and I instantly fell in love with Dr Martinez. She was South American and had a hugely welcoming disposition and a graceful demeanour. She seemed to be full of life and hope, with her shiny brown hair that spilled voluptuously over her shoulders, and her rich, almost edible accent. I immediately felt comfortable with her and trusted her. She inspired untold confidence in both of us. Based on no background knowledge, I was ready to believe she had all the answers. Of course, sadly, not only did she not have any answers, but she also irritatingly typed continuously throughout the meeting.

I couldn't imagine what on earth was so important that it distracted her from her young patient and her parents sitting right in front of her. It was only later that I realised that she was being super-efficient and typing up all the information we were giving her, as well as simultaneously noting down her plans for going forward. In the letter we subsequently received, there were encouraging remarks that:

> Alice was feeding normally and had had no significant illnesses. No known allergies, on no medications, she sleeps well and eats well. On examination: she is a lovely girl who played happily on her mother's lap. She does have a divergent alternating squint, but has a full range of eye movements (up and down) with no nystagmus.

I had been going to London very frequently, probably once or twice a week. Alice had had most of the tests for all the main illnesses, blood issues and genetic problems that would typically be the cause of the delays that she was experiencing. She had the 'normal' female chromosomes and the fragile X syndrome was discounted. The tests for the myotonic dystrophy gene and the MECP2 gene were both negative. The neurometabolic investigations and electroencephalogram (EEG) were all under way.

A month or so after we first saw Dr Martinez, our fascinating London paediatric neurologist, she wrote to us to say:

> I now have the results of most investigations. She still has increased plasma lactate, but the results also suggested that she might have a

> generalised peroxisomal disorder with moderately elevated C26/C22 ratio and C24/C22 ratio, plus moderately elevated pristinate and phytanate. It was suggested that we should repeat these tests, plus do plasmalogen analysis. We did not manage to do MPS screen or transferrin glycoforms. I would prefer for Alice to be seen by Prof. Clayton and he could organise then the repeat tests and the ones that have not been carried out. She had slightly increased proline, high TSH, and the MRI showed a lack of white muscle bulk with a thin corpus callosum.

In the above paragraph, the only words that were English to me, not having a medical background, was the doctor's reference to Alice needing to see 'Prof. Clayton… repeat tests'.

As it turned out, this was only the first of the many difficult moments in my life with Alice. Professor Clayton was not just a local professor; he was based at Great Ormond Street Hospital. We saw him promptly, and he conducted all the necessary tests, repeating the ones that Dr Martinez had done and indicated as vital. They indicated a peroxisomal disorder. This meant, in non-medical language, that the child in question (i.e. Alice) couldn't correctly process fats. We understood that these fats would become like a poison in her system. We were, however, tentatively told that this diagnosis was probably a long shot and certainly wasn't conclusive, since Alice didn't have any of the usual dysmorphic features typically associated with a peroxisomal disorder. Professor Clayton explained that this particular syndrome was usually characterised by a known 'birth look', in the same way that Down's children have specific facial characteristics.

Even though it looked unlikely that Alice had this syndrome based on all that the professor could see in her physically, the blood results spoke otherwise. Professor Clayton felt strongly enough about the probability that he decided to do more invasive tests, including a skin biopsy on her upper arm. He said that, due to her blood results, he was ninety-eight per cent sure that she had this condition. Compassionately, he told us that he didn't want to go into details about the condition as it would be too distressing and because he felt it was still a long shot, given the way she looked. Honestly, I think he was more than a little surprised by what he was seeing in her blood results. Luckily, in his opinion, there seemed little point in him delving into the details of a condition that might not be relevant to Alice.

We now live in a world with the internet, and so naturally, as soon as I got home, I Googled 'peroxisomal disorder'. This proved very unhelpful, to state the obvious. This was one of only two times in my life as a Christian that I felt God almost physically put His protection over me. Every time I tried to imagine what Alice having the condition would mean for me, for her, for the boys and for us as a family, I was almost physically unable to do so. It was as if, every time I tried to turn my head to the possible horror of what might be on the horizon, I was blocked. As if someone had physically put my head in a position

New addition to the family,
Rutland, September 2006.

Learning to sit up
with Amanda's help,
Rutland, April 2008.

Riding on Toby with Janet, Copthill Farm, September 2008.

Learning to walk at home in the kitchen, Rutland, January 2009.

Alice in the garden at home with her brothers,
Rutland, July 2009.

Fun times with mum in Africa,
September, 2009.

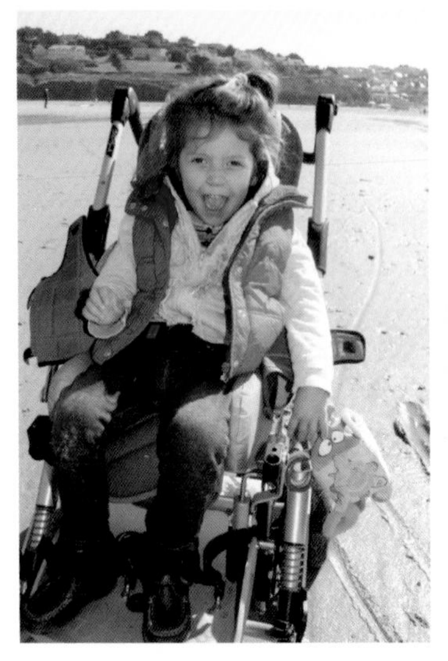

Left: Polzeath Beach, Cornwall, April, 2010
Right: Just learnt to walk on my own with Mum, Kay and Matthew standing by! Bath, Valley View Barn, May 2010.

The Pool, Trevose, Cornwall, August, 2011.

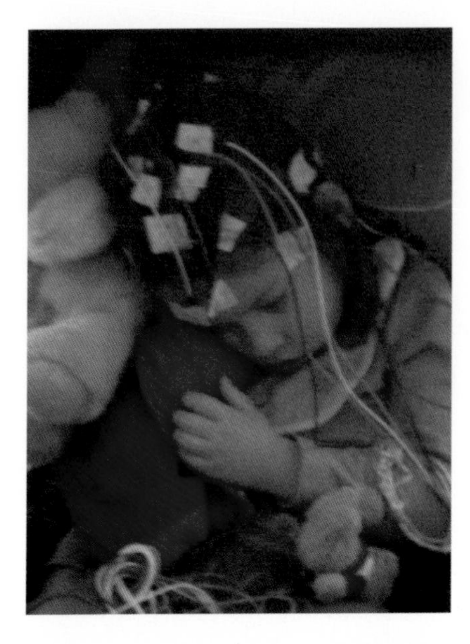

One of many
EEG tests RUH,
Bath, April 2011.

At 'work' listening to complex classical music,
Trebetherick, Cornwall, August, 2011.

Sunset walk with Mum and Dad
Constantine, Cornwall, August 2011.

Left: Relaxing at home in Valley View Barn, Bath, September 2011; Right: First day at Three Ways School, Odd down, Somerset, Bath, September 2011.

Bristol Royal Hospital for Children, with
David's parents and the five of us, April, 2012.

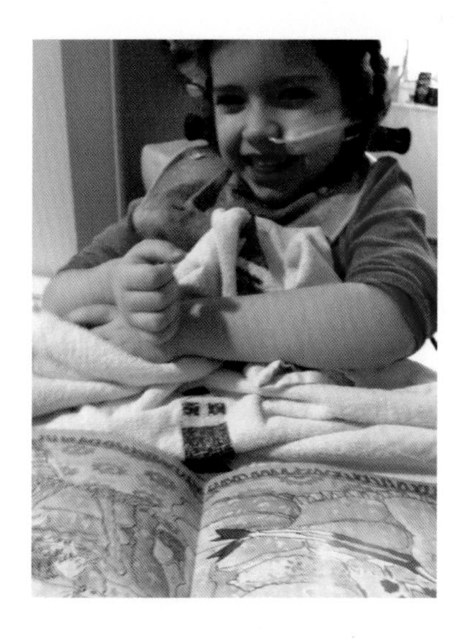

Happy moments at the
Children's Hospital,
Bristol with mum and
the nurses, May, 2012.

Burial at Hinton Charterhouse, Bath, July 2012.

Alice's Gravestone, Hinton Charterhouse, Bath, 2015.

where I was only able to look forward or away from my present reality, and every time I tried to turn my thoughts in towards the fear, I was prevented from doing so.

Strangely, after six long, nerve-racking weeks, the biopsy results came back clear. So the next time we saw Professor Clayton, he said that life could continue as 'normal' as Alice didn't have this disorder.

I have to say that there is a part of me that is 'enjoying' writing this, because I have managed to condense six weeks of pure agony into a few simple paragraphs of unemotional prose. Professor Clayton did say that I shouldn't be surprised if Alice started having seizures. He said it would be common and relatively likely that a child 'like Alice' would develop epilepsy, and that I should be vigilant for any signs of seizures or 'absences', which are seizures that can be very easy to miss. As I understood it, during an 'absent' seizure, the child might appear to be looking into the distance or daydreaming, but internally their brain would be screaming.

Subsequently, I did look for signs and episodes like this, but early on, I never saw any. It was only much later, when the seizures became intense, that it was apparent, and not only to me.

I have one very clear memory from shortly after our meeting with the Great Ormond Street professor about the possible peroxisomal disorder. Alice and I were sitting on the sloping lawn outside our house in Rutland with

Janet, Kay and Amanda beside us. Janet was busy fussing and placing the pillows and blankets we needed around or over us. Kay was providing us with hot and cold drinks and biscuits, and Amanda, as Alice's attentive nanny, was checking Alice didn't need anything else. Janet had just carefully propped up the ever-smiling Alice with a pillow and cushions, as she had just started to tip over, having begun to randomly lose her sitting skills.

It was a bright, sunny day, and for some reason, I had a peculiar feeling that I was in a lumpish scene in an old budget movie. If I had been, the background music might have been a violin solo, or an oboe playing a mournful overture. My film was lit by a hazy, warm day, highlighted by the soft light of the afternoon sun. The camera in my head zooms in on a mother, gazing out into the distance, a small train quietly clanking through the trees past the end of her garden, which it had done perfectly on cue. In this film, the mother (me) was explaining to her companions (Janet, Kay and Amanda) that her daughter (Alice)'s recent diagnosis meant she would probably not see her fifth birthday. Cue more sorrowful violins.

As I could tell by this stupid 'film' in my head, I felt incredibly self-conscious and more self-aware than I had probably ever done. This was during the six weeks when we were waiting for the results of the tests for peroxisomal disorder. I was about to tell some of those closest to me the dreadful news about the possibility that Alice had a limited future, and would die early. I felt my facial expressions, such as they were, were artificial. It all felt like make-believe, which is doubtless why I had a ridiculous self-conscious feeling of being in a film.

Tragically, I was not in a film. If I had been, then the whole thing would have been fictional, instead of real life: Alice's life and my own. As I shared my news about the possible peroxisomal disorder, no one spoke, but there was a lot of compassionate nodding from my companions.

This news turned out to be no news at all (fake news, as President Trump might say), since Alice was cleared of having the peroxisomal disorder. The irony is that she died close to her sixth birthday – as she would have done had she had this syndrome. In the hospital, she had also been put on a ketogenic diet, which is a very high-fat diet, to try to control the epilepsy which she apparently didn't have! Evidently, she also didn't have the peroxisomal disorder. Several times I had flagged all this confusing information up to the doctors and nurses, but in truth, no one knew what was best for her.

I held on tightly to the comforting words just after the ones Marie-Louise had highlighted in my Bible. In Psalm 139:16 it says:

> Your eyes saw my unformed body; all the
> days ordained for me were written in Your
> book before one of them came to be.

No one had made a mistake; everyone was trying their best. Alice lived all the days she was meant to and then died on the day that no one could possibly have foreseen.

17

Schools

When we were still in Rutland, we knew we had to start planning to move from the house we'd thought of as our home for the rest of our lives. Alice was still relatively well, albeit disabled, but I was aware that I needed more support, advice and, most importantly, professionals who had been trained to help a child 'like Alice'.

Before we discovered the unsurpassable Three Ways School in Bath, we had travelled around the country trying to find a school that could take Alice and would offer the most opportunities for her. We visited many schools in Rutland, Cambridgeshire, Leicestershire and Lincolnshire, near to where we were living at the time. Then we looked further afield. We searched near my in-laws' home in Buckinghamshire, near my father in Berkshire and Oxfordshire, and looked at schools near the one we'd previously enrolled Ben in, also knowing that the time for homeschooling the boys was running out, and we might have to look for a school for them too.

The boys were getting older, and we both felt they needed a school that could provide them with the breadth of experiences and education that is now available in most schools. We also wanted the range of different sports and extracurricular activities that I could not provide. At this point, my health was still stable, but I knew it was time for a change.

Our primary concern in all this, however, was our daughter. We were ready to move anywhere that would benefit her. Luckily, as I was still homeschooling the boys and David was running his own business, we were free to up sticks anywhere and at any point. It's interesting how decisions become so much clearer the more desperate the situation.

Selling our house was a small, but cripplingly expensive problem in the whole process. We'd bought this house, our first home, at the height of the property market, and now we had to move during the property slump following the well-noted global financial crisis. We ended up selling at an excruciating loss, so it was a much more significant than expected glitch for our next move.

We had looked at all the schools in Rutland that were appropriate for a disabled child and, sadly, had ruled out every single one. Amongst the criteria we were looking for, which in fact every school failed to meet, was the opportunity for me to accompany my daughter into the classroom. Bar none, every school refused my presence. I understood that schools, especially those for children with special needs, have stringent rules and regulations, but if Alice couldn't go to school with me, then I would have chosen to keep her at home.

This was a very different prospect to schooling Ben and Matthew. If either of the boys were unhappy with anything, we could chat it through together and work out compromises or more preferable solutions. But Alice was not the same. Having had three years as her primary carer, I was particularly protective of her and conscious of her insufficiencies. Her inability to communicate at all made it very hard for me to let her go. I was particularly observant of her complex needs, and I didn't relish the thought of collecting her from school and then wondering why she was upset or fractious.

If I was always going to be with her, I knew I would be able to understand the reasons why she was upset or unhappy. I could be her private physician, with all the information I needed to make my diagnosis at my fingertips. However diligent a school might be, I couldn't expect them to watch her the way I would watch her, or to be able to interpret her behaviour in the way that I would.

All the same, I do appreciate that schools for children with special needs find it easier to work when parents are out of sight and therefore out of mind. No school could be expected to manage the parent or carer as well as all the other paraphernalia that each child travels with, just as no school should be expected to cope with all the emotional baggage, as well as the practical luggage, that comes with a parent of a special needs child.

Alice had no preschooling, and I was still taking her to mother and baby groups. However, while all the babies were growing up and moving on, Alice and I were still in the same groups, frustratingly stuck doing the same things, looking older and more and more out of place. I was getting tired, with a few grey hairs to frame my increasingly wrinkled face. 'The Wheels on the Bus' were still going round and round, yet Alice was bigger and was becoming more and more obviously different from the other children. I was looking for a change, and for an organisation that could help me get the best out of her.

While we were on the hunt for somewhere appropriate for Alice, we went to Bath and saw the incredible Three Ways School, and met the headmistress, Julie Dyer, who was one hundred per cent dedicated to the children in her care. She'd helped design the school, together with the architect, with the children's needs at the forefront of her planning. She immediately agreed to let me stay in school with Alice and be her carer, her helper, her friend, her voice. I, her biggest fan, her champion, her adoring mother, was allowed to stay with her. I was also able to nominate another carer to go with her if I needed to be elsewhere. This was enough to trigger our move to Bath. The only thing we needed to do was to make sure we got our CRB (now DBS) certificates.

It's not surprising that I still have a genuine love for Three Ways, as all my experiences there confirmed my hopes. My only sadness is that Alice only managed one term there before she had to go into hospital. Then she died, and so never went back.

At this time, I had also accepted the fact that I could no longer be my sons' teacher. Home-tutoring Ben and Matthew meant I was spreading myself too thinly. It was time for them to go to school and get the best education from people who were qualified to do the job. This was no longer me. David had gone to meet the head of the boys' school, Monkton, while I stayed in a pub nearby with the three children. He came back full of excitement for the two boys and the news that we could meet some parents, Paddy and Susannah, who also had a daughter at Three Ways School. We met them, and, when we subsequently moved to Bath, they became good friends of ours.

The classrooms at Three Ways were huge, the communal areas big enough for all the latest pushchairs, as well as all the children's specific tools for their complex needs: oxygen tanks, breathing accessories, standing frames, electric wheelchairs, Jenx chairs, and so many more things. The list of activities the school was able to give the children was immense. There was a water mobility pool, a multisensory studio, green screens and iPads all crying out to be used and enjoyed. When Alice started at Bath Opportunity Preschool (BOP), next door to Three Ways, they also had access to the pool. I had not expected her to have to join the preschool, but because of her September birthday, she couldn't go straight into Three Ways and would have to wait until she was five. I spent many a wet afternoon in the pool, having lots of fun and games with a group of children, hoping that none of them would throw up, which would mean that we would all have to evacuate quickly and everything be washed and sterilised!

The building itself was monolithic. It was brand new, and the classrooms were light and bright, most with floor-to-ceiling windows and doors with plenty of space for the kids and an accompanying adult to get through. Outside the classroom where Alice spent her first and only term, there was a playground, which was a small, safe area leading onto the much larger playground for the rest of the pupils. There were climbing frames, walkways, large tyres swinging from tastefully made wooden beams. I was totally in love with this school. There was everything, and so much more than I could possibly have wished for.

I haven't mentioned any of the staff members. I should have done, as Julie Dyer's leadership and example meant that Three Ways was a very caring and exceptionally professional outfit. I would have trusted anyone there one hundred per cent.

I was completely sold on this school, but we still had to face the battle to have Alice accepted. We filled in copious lengthy forms, which I hated, and I also had to have her independently assessed. I was unnecessarily nervous that she wouldn't meet the criteria for being accepted into this school; needless to say, it was never going to be an issue. She was given a place, but not until we'd filled in every form and seen everyone who could write a report backing our belief that this school was necessary for Alice.

Incidentally, this was also only after David and I had had to sit through a tense, drawn-out meeting with the local council and persuade them that there was no way Alice could be part of the traditional education system. As a child who needed 24/7 care, we argued that she was never going to be able to 'fit in' with 'normal' life in a mainstream school.

Ben started at his school, located nearby, in January when he was eight-and-a-half, and he was ready. He waltzed in, practically running! He was thrilled, which was a huge relief, especially since his unhappiness at school was the reason I had homeschooled him and Matthew in the first place. Matthew was six-and-a-half and not so happy about going to school, but fortunately he coped with the change very bravely.

Alice started at BOP with Three Ways to look forward to, and our family began a completely new life in Bath.

18

Bath

Before we had moved from the house in Rutland to go to Bath, I'd arranged with our nanny, Liz, that Alice would stay with her and her partner for three days while the boys and I went to the new house to get everything ready. In her typical and generous way, Kay had also offered her invaluable practical motherly help, packing boxes and supporting me in yet another move. Liz was super-organised, sensible and had lived with me through the days of the demanding physio exercises, the painting mess, the Riding for the Disabled mornings and many more of the challenging times I'd been through with Alice.

When I had considered the multitude of things I'd have to do in Bath – the inevitable ensuing tedium of a family move – the thought of dragging Alice around and worrying about her and her comfort was overwhelming.

I knew I would have to cope with this move mostly on my own, and I was very aware that our daughter was a full-time job without the added pressure of furnishing and filling an empty house – not to mention filling an empty fridge. Not only that, I also had the task of settling the boys into school with the whole unfamiliar concept of a school day. David would be at work, and, when at home in Bath, he would be even further away from all the places he needed to be for work. We knew it was a genuine sacrifice that we were both going to have to make, he especially.

We had made up our minds and decided that, with all the practicalities of the move, the sensible decision was to leave Alice safely with Liz. It seemed an inspired idea. Liz had been working for us for about eighteen months, and she'd been a very safe pair of hands for all of us. Alice loved her, and she loved Alice. Liz was very gracious about the changes our move to Bath would mean for her, for which we were extremely thankful. So, having decided to leave Alice with Liz, we set off for Bath. I phoned Liz over the few days that we were away and the feedback was good. I didn't feel there was any cause for alarm, and Liz was confident that both she and Alice were coping seamlessly.

On the prearranged morning, three days after we'd left Alice with Liz, David set off to meet them halfway between Rutland and Bath. It had been snowing heavily, and Liz was worried that she wouldn't be able to get to our new house to meet us. We had a four-wheel drive, which would make it easier for us to tackle the slopes in Bath, so David agreed to meet her halfway.

He successfully collected Alice, said thank you and goodbye to Liz again, and arrived safely back at the house we were renting – a recently converted pig barn. David and I had decided that we would all go out to the local pub for lunch, which meant I wouldn't have to cook and clean up. I had missed Alice, and couldn't wait to see her and take her round our new home. I was looking forward to showing her her wardrobe with clothes proudly hanging up in the only cupboard we had in the house. Then I wanted to remind her of her familiar cot and cuddly toys, all of whom, I wanted to assure her, had been missing her. I wanted her to see just how close her room was to ours, explaining that I would be able to hear the moment she woke up and uttered a sound. After that, I had planned to let her see her bathroom, where the bubble game and her plastic toys were ready, and where I was expecting she would later have a warm, very bubbly bath. I had the whole day mapped out beautifully for us both.

It wasn't long after David walked into the house, carefully carrying Alice, that I realised that all was not well with our precious daughter. From the moment I saw her, she was screaming and crying inconsolably. I had never seen her so fractious. She was apoplectic. Her little face was creased with confusion, and her body was rigid. I had no idea what was wrong. I knew as a parent, and especially as a parent of a child such as Alice, that I had to use my observational skills to assess what might be causing her to behave so uncharacteristically.

As a rule, I was the main authority on matters relating to Alice, but this time I had no idea what to do. I quickly scanned my mental 'info disk'. She'd been asleep in Liz's car, before David had met them and collected her to bring her to Bath, so she wasn't tired. I made sure her nappy had been changed, so she wasn't uncomfortable. She didn't want a drink, so not thirsty. She refused food, so she wasn't hungry. She was warm and comfortable, so it wasn't obviously physical. All the possible causes of her distress had been discounted, and yet still Alice continued her frenzied tantrum.

Then suddenly it hit me like a punch in the face. I knew with crystal clarity what was wrong. Alice was utterly furious with me for leaving her in an unfamiliar environment, and, more than that, there had been no discussion or explanation. I had left her with Liz without even having the decency to clear it with her or even mention it first. By this time, I knew her well enough to know that she understood much more than she was able to convey. Even though Liz had been her nanny for the past year and a half, she had been left in an unfamiliar home and for an unknown time frame. For all Alice knew, she might have been moving in with Liz forever, never again to see her mother and father or her brothers. At her age and level of development, of course, these would be subconscious fears; however, it was something that had disturbed her.

It was a thoughtless thing for me to have done. I'd left her behind for my own convenience, with the excuse that it would be less disruptive for her. Perfectly reasonable behaviour that, as adults, we would accept. For a child like Alice, who couldn't understand what was going on, it might possibly have been terrifying. Would I have done that to Ben or Matthew? No. Never. Not in a million years.

I vowed then that I would never underestimate Alice again. She was a quiet little soul, but with a massive, inaudible voice. Fully, an oxymoron. Hadn't I learnt this in South Africa? She demanded to be treated in the same way as a child who can verbally explain what is right and what is wrong, and should be considered in the same way.

It was another turning point for me. As soon as I apologised and explained to her how ashamed I was of my behaviour, and how deeply sorry I was, she calmed down. Her peace and forgiveness were instantaneous.

Alice was three years and four months old when she started at Three Ways nursery. The 'Pig Barn' was the ideal house for us. The layout was perfect. The boys would be upstairs in ginormous individual rooms at either end of the building. Ridiculously, they each had their own en suite and were distantly connected to each other by a long, wide corridor, perfect for indoor cricket. It looked as if the architect must have had a lot of fun designing this unusual house. This interconnecting passage overlooked the main room downstairs, and Alice, David and I had our bedrooms downstairs, where there were also two bathrooms. There was another bedroom, which we didn't need, so David used this as his office on the odd occasion he worked from home. It was a rental property which had never been used before and, although it was newly finished and spotlessly clean, it had never been lived in and was grossly lacking in some of the basics – things that we often take for granted, like cupboards and shelves.

When we moved into the Pig Barn, which by this time had been given the more acceptable name of Valley View Barn, we had very little of the furniture that most couples accumulate over the years. Things that are usually carted from home to home, such as chairs and tables, lights, a television and a sofa. We did have a few useful hand-me-downs as my father had downsized a couple of years before and had needed to find a home for some of the possessions he no longer had room for. We knew we still needed some essentials to add to our diverse mix of furniture to match our eclectic family and dogs.

Valley View Barn, however, was jam-packed with toys, toys and more toys; teddies and baby teddies and learning tools for Alice. It felt like a new beginning, with the smell of a fresh coat of paint and change in everything. We now had a school for the boys to go to; their school uniforms hanging up, labelled and ready to wear. Alice was enrolled in a preschool (the one attached to Three Ways), and I was swept up in all the anticipation of what this would mean for her. She would have a team of suitably qualified and fully trained staff to work with her and to help me.

We also had an athletic and sometimes neurotically yappy Jack Russell, who fitted neatly into our somewhat disparate and chaotic lives. I had also managed to negotiate buying a Labrador within the first month of moving to Bath. I am never one to see my limits, but Matthew had been waiting patiently for 'his' dog and Pepper, a soft and gentle black Labrador, turned up at just the right time for him as well as for all of us.

Soon after we moved, when we were able to assess our living requirements, we went to a Swedish furniture shop (which also sells meatballs) whose name is now virtually a swear word in our house. David and I had a severe marital moment there, and, I have to say, it was not an enjoyable one.

At the time, David was in the middle of an important business deal, and we still had no money. He decided he wanted to come to IKEA to help me furnish the house, and, naturally, we were doing it all on a fraying shoestring. My questions, like, "Which cupboard?" or "What about that one?" were met with raised eyebrows and comments like, "Let me have a... hold on, I thought we'd discussed this; we can't... just coming, let me have a look..."

It didn't take me too long to realise that David was not only having a conversation with me about cupboards, but was also in the midst of a crucial negotiation with a work colleague on the phone. I had to guess which of us he was talking to when he said, "That's excellent, perfect."

All I could focus on was shelves, cupboards, curtains or blinds, some beds, bedside tables, and getting all this before four o'clock, when the boys needed picking up from school. We had also left Alice at home with someone I barely knew.

Angrily, I thought to myself, *David, if you didn't want to come, then why come? I know you meant to be helpful but why on earth are you here, especially when you evidently don't want to be?*

Despite his good intentions, David was decidedly less than helpful. I honestly believe that surviving a trip to the above-mentioned Swedish furniture emporium is as good as any marriage preparation course. If you make it through this test, then you'll surely weather anything else married life might throw at you. The Swedish Furniture Emporium Test, hitherto known as the SFET test, should be obligatory for all engaged couples. Add into the mix of shopping and choosing furniture, negotiating the purchase of a business or a property and see how your relationship copes? It's just a random suggestion.

Despite some smothered threats and unfriendly glances, we didn't end up filing for divorce; it was cheaper to buy a cupboard and a bed and some chests of drawers for the boys. We still had the unenviable job of assembling them once we got home, though. These are more memories that are best left in the drawer marked: *JUNK! DO NOT OPEN!*

Fortunately, in our new home, we had a good working kitchen and lovely, clean, brand-new modern bathrooms, which, along with the Swedish furniture, albeit tainted by a rather pathetic argument, were all we needed for the time being. We had an incomparable view over the valley looking up to the south of Bath. Unfortunately, the postage-stamp-sized garden had not yet been introduced to any green fingers, so we couldn't see much of this outstanding view due to the thick, unkempt hedge blocking the panoramic fields beyond. This meant we were unable to enjoy the light and impressive beauty around us. We had brought our trampoline from Rutland, and the boys still enjoyed tumbling around on it and chucking a tennis ball to each other in directions that would force the recipient to fling themselves wildly into the protective netting in order to catch it. We would sometimes all clamber onto the trampoline and join in with the fun and games together. Alice loved her time with her brothers as we all giggled at the static-electricity-induced punk hairstyles we were all sporting. We had no spare money to invest on our garden, and I never cut the overgrowth down – the hedge, not the hair – which was a shame. Alice's needs and the boys' schooling were causing enough financial distress without lavishing funds on a garden we didn't own.

The house was in a rambling hamlet overlooking fields where some very highly-strung racehorses were housed. In inclement weather, these horses were kept in the stables close to our home. The other days, they were put out into the fields, where they kept the grass looking like it had been mown. They were stunning beasts, and our only problem with them was when they were ridden through the lanes in the mornings and afternoons, slowing down the traffic when we were on the school run. It was mostly the trainers who, when they weren't glued to their phones, caused angst, as they glared daggers at us drivers trapped inside our cars. Mostly young women, they were too inexperienced to understand parental anxiety; trying to get children to school on time, or back home in time for tea and homework before bed, was not on their radar.

We lived at the top of a long, precipitous single track with only a handful of passing places. My mother-in-law had a problem with this hill, as did both of us. I'm sure she wouldn't mind me saying that she used to hate reversing. To be fair to her, this was a viciously steep slope. So steep that it was virtually impossible, if you were reversing, to see the road behind you in the rear-view mirror. The driver was usually only just able to catch a glimpse of the whimsical clouds as they joyfully drifted about in the sky above, oblivious to the tense situation below.

I have got to know David's mother, Anne, so much better in the years since Alice died. We now live close to each other, and I have time that I didn't have before. This means I can invest in relationships that had been on the shelf for the time being, and, despite her valiant efforts, ours was sadly one that suffered. This little 'reversing car' snag in our life in Bath is funny now that Anne and I can laugh about it. However, at the time it was not very amusing for anyone. It was one of those rather tense, unspoken inconveniences. One side of the track, masquerading as a road, was a sheer drop into the fields below. The overall stress of this was magnified whenever the dreaded horses were on the road, sneezing, snorting and defecating en route.

There was one infamous occasion when my mother-in-law was in her car, her husband at her side and driving down the hill along one of the sharpest bends. As luck would have it, she came across a horse whose rider was also holding another, extremely lively, tethered horse on a lead rein. There was a stand-off while both women glared at each other, neither willing to be the one to give way. I can't remember the exact result, but suffice to say my mother-in-law was rumoured to have been heard muttering under her breath, "I don't *do* reverse."

Apart from this minor vehicular inconvenience, we mostly loved our time living in Bath. What's not to love in the architecture and beauty of this city?

Anne has a fantastic sense of humour as well as a stoical strength of character. I have so appreciated and admired all she has uncomplainingly faced in her life. She has been an enormous strength and comfort to us over the years, most notably since her husband, dear Anthony's, death, which followed less than a year after Alice's. I realise I haven't mentioned either of these beautiful individuals much, but this perhaps illustrates just how preoccupied I was with our daughter, and how many of my minutes, hours and days she managed to fill.

Part Three

2009–2019

19

ABA and Tutors

Soon after we arrived in Bath, we engaged tutors to help me run the applied behaviour analysis (ABA) teaching programme. We had just begun the new technique of communication with Alice, called Makaton, which included teaching her to communicate with us using basic sign language, and Mr Tumble was an excellent resource for us. For those whose children missed out on Mr Tumble (and our boys only learnt about him through Alice), he was (and still is) an imaginative source of fun and amusement.

Mr Tumble is a character created by Justin Fletcher, an English comedian, children's television presenter and actor on the BBC's preschool channel CBeebies. He will often speak, sing, dress up and perform in various self-created and amusing roles. He mainly specialises in slapstick comedy, and this works well with special needs children. His show, *Something Special*, transfixed Alice.

I often used some of the Makaton sign language to communicate with the boys when we were out and about, or when I needed them to hear me in noisy situations. Useful signs like *Be quiet*, or *Do you want something to eat?*

It was in Bath that I first met Scarlet. Very soon after our move, I had heard a good deal about this fabulous mother from various school mums. I had never met anyone with her energy, her engagement, her influence on my life. She was a larger-than-life character, very smart, and not one to hide her many talents. Scarlet was stunning, with a memorable face and long, black, immensely curly hair (both traits which were closely mirrored by her two black poodles, one handbag size and the other a tall, striking standard poodle).

Scarlet wasn't shy when it came to trying to educate those around her in her way of thinking. This is not meant to be a backhanded criticism. Far from it: for me she was a tour de force for change, enlightenment and growth. Her son, Jack, was slightly older than Ben and was at that time a pupil at the boys' new school in Bath. Jack had an autistic spectrum disorder, and I had heard that Scarlet had been treating him herself, under the auspices of specialist doctors, with biomedical intervention and behavioural strategies which, together with many other disciplines, had dramatically changed his behaviour. Together with doctors specialising in bio- and functional medicine, she had managed to bring Jack out of his silence and solitude.

I didn't know Jack then, and I have only ever really known him from a distance, but I do know enough to be confident that what happened to this child is real. I've seen Jack standing on a stage at school, speaking in public, eloquently introducing his brother, Teddy, who was playing the guitar in a solo piece. This could not have been invented, embellished or faked. Jack stood confidently in front of everyone, smiling, his eyes shining with pride.

Having heard that he'd started his life in the preschool that Alice was now at (BOP, the one that led to Three Ways), it seemed nothing short of a miracle. This was precisely the kind of miracle I was looking for. I saw this young man as a lifeline. Here was my road to wholeness for Alice. And, in Jack's mother, I found a kindred spirit. Scarlet was someone who, like me, didn't know the meaning of the phrase 'to give up'. She was someone who would listen to me and could hopefully show me the way forward. It seemed then that she was the one person who could help me find a cure for Alice.

Scarlet had encouraged me to try ABA myself as she had used it successfully to teach Jack to do things that hadn't come naturally to him. Her son, now a teenager at a mainstream school, was then busy focusing on his GCSEs rather than his difficulties. The ABA programme had helped him not only to understand the basics of life, but also the subtle clues in human behaviour that most of us pick up naturally. Simple things, like smiling at others when they smile at you; the basic innate things that can also be lost on many 'normal' children until they are a little older, or until encouraged by their parents! He also learnt other things, such as remembering to say 'thank you', and stopping to listen to others. Having seen this work so successfully for her son, Scarlet suggested I get in touch with a behavioural analyst called Katie, who could help establish a programme that would be suitable for Alice.

Luckily, Katie had a window in her busy schedule. She turned out to be a charming and very experienced consultant and, even though she hadn't treated a child like Alice before, or indeed encountered a child with such profound difficulties, she took us on. It wasn't unusual for this teaching programme to be used outside of the specific parameters of autism. With no diagnosis for Alice, these techniques seemed to be a good start.

Katie was one of those rare gems on this earth who approached her often quite challenging work with good humour. She obviously loved working with children and nothing was too much trouble for her. Her work was intense, but she made it fun as well. After we had met for the first time, she got straight to work with Alice.

An initial aim with ABA is to 'positively pair' things that the child likes doing with things they either don't like or can't see the value of doing, or, more accurately for us, don't know how to do. This tool works well for developmentally delayed children, such as those with an autistic spectrum disorder. Children with these difficulties can sometimes be very exacting about the things they do or don't want to do. By helping them understand the underlying motivation and purpose in learning some of these skills, eventually, they can take pleasure in doing certain things that they'd otherwise find stressful or pointless.

For a child like Alice, it was definitely helpful. Perhaps we should all be trained in this last skill! Like most people, there were and still are so many things in my life I don't want to do, but know I have to. If I took the time to understand the underlying value of my actions, or if there was a treat at the end of each unpleasant job, maybe that would help. I suppose that's what we call 'wages'.

Katie drew up a lengthy assessment of where Alice was on the average scale of development. She was extremely low down on the scale of communication and could barely do anything that was considered normal. She couldn't talk, point or motion towards anything in a way that anyone could recognise. She could, however, smile like no one else. I wasn't put off by her difficulties; a little flummoxed, perhaps.

We all have to start somewhere and, having reached nowhere in the outside lane, at least I felt we were going to do something that might help Alice to communicate. We could then get out of the slow lane going in the wrong direction and take a diversion to a more fulfilling end – last to the finish line would be just fine.

In order to fill the week, and to help me to practise the ABA techniques, we employed two tutors to work to

Katie's recommendations, both of whom were psychology graduates. Each would do one or two days per week, under the supervision of Katie, who would consult one day a month for ongoing assessment, tutor training, and to move Alice's targets forward. Rosie and Juliet were two of the first who arrived to help us out. They were hugely enthusiastic and only too happy to be shown what to do and to learn the ABA teaching programme.

I first met Rosie on her bike outside our house, and frankly I wondered how on earth she had managed the hill, as I'd never seen a cyclist attempt it before! She was efficient and very bright. Juliet arrived in a more traditional manner in her car. She was always cheerful and confident in all she did with our daughter. She often went to BOP or took Alice to a playgroup; then when Alice was old enough, she would take her to her 'grown-up' school. Later on, she helped us out with overnight stays at the hospital. Juliet was always serene, and nothing ever seemed to be too much trouble. I loved having her at home.

The other days of the week would be completed by me, or sometimes not at all. At any one point, I always had a team of two to work with us, as well as an occasional visit from Katie. This is where Jenny also filled a gap. She had worked for Scarlet when teaching Jack the ABA techniques. She was happy to cover many of my Saturday times with Alice, as I was finding it harder and harder to meet the boys' demands alongside our daughter's needs. She was always cheerful and fun to spend time with; all of us loved the time we had with her.

As an aside, we were only able t
money that was generously lent to us b
were also fortunate that we had a particula
colleague of David's who cared about our situatio
practical way. We were very grateful for this suppo ,
thankfully, were able to pay them all back in due course.

The ABA programme consisted of sheets and sheets of exercises to be filled in and marked carefully with Alice's achievements or lack thereof. She never got much further than the very first few sections on the sheets, and, depressingly, these were marked with lots of 'X's, indicating skills not learnt.

But honestly, it didn't seem to matter as Alice was so happy and enjoyed the intense interaction with her tutors or me. I'm calling these girls 'tutors', but it might be more accurate to describe them as friends or loving aunties as well as paediatric psychology professionals. All, bar none, were wholly dedicated to the teaching scheme and at the same time devoted to Alice. They watched over her with tenderness as well as persevering with her on the lengthy, complicated programme. I believe ABA is mainstream in this country now and is partially offered on the NHS, depending on the county. It was first trialled as an aid for autistic children in America, and I started experimenting with it when it was still in its infancy in this country.

Scarlet has remained a friend whom I will always respect. She came to Alice's funeral despite her dislike of both religion and particularly sad occasions. I read in: *Behind the Scenes at the Museum* by Kate Atkinson: 'The future is like a cupboard full of light and all you have to do is find the key that opens the door.' Scarlet was going to be my key, if there was ever going to be one, to let the light in for Alice.

When we lived in Bath, our lives became filled with people who were in their early twenties. After a short while, I hired Charlotte to help with the cleaning and looking after the boys, as well as to carry out light work with Alice. Charlotte fell in love with Alice – everyone did. Alice was like a warm and vibrant shining light that drew everyone close. Charlotte worked diligently and kindly for me until Alice died and we left Bath. I had so many lovely girls around me: Katie, Charlotte, all the people who worked on ABA with Alice – Jenny (though not in her twenties, she worked as if she could still be!), Naomi, Rosie, Juliet, Anna and Hazel – and all the others who came in and out of our house. They could only really be found all together after Alice died, but they knew of each other. This was the Bath version of the Rutland 'Team Alice', a phrase coined by her physio, Sarah, which had in those days included the speech and language, physio and occupational therapists, as well as Amanda and then Liz. With no hands-on family to help me, these girls were invaluable and hugely appreciated.

Apparently, most kids laugh over three hundred times a day. Statistics say that, as an adult, I should laugh 150 times, but I sometimes struggle to manage a single weak smile, let alone a hearty laugh. Katie was an adult who laughed easily, certainly over 150 times a day, and I longed for the joy and hope that she shone into our house. I love the fact that both boys remember Alice as smiling a lot, and, surprisingly, both remember her laughing too. My memory is that she didn't often laugh as such, although she did always have a ready smile. But why would I disabuse them of such happy memories? Having read Rosie's note, which she wrote for me included at the end of this book, she remembers her laughing and giggling too. It seems that perhaps I'm the one with the erroneous memories.

We did need a team to care for Alice as well as for me, David and the boys. We were building something special; a community held together with love and purpose. Anyone who wanted to help us, we welcomed. We needed support, and the people who answered our ads and pleas were embraced with unconditionally open arms. Perhaps this book is simply one I wanted to write in order to honour and thank all those who worked with us and cared for our daughter.

I don't think I truly understood the love that Alice's tutors and carers felt for her, or the joy and unconditional love she fed them daily. It was probably only near the end of Alice's life that I fully appreciated the positive impact she'd had on all those around her. Only when one of her tutors wanted to come to the hospital twice in her last few days, to say an emotional goodbye, did I fully appreciate the extent of the impression she'd made on the lives of many of those around her.

On my long list of things to do, the next thing to try with Alice was potty training. Having been encouraged by Janet in Rutland, what seemed like a million light years ago, I decided to help Alice grow and change as a 'normal' child might do, and the next thing was to try and 'toilet' her.

When we were still living in Rutland, Janet had suggested teaching Alice to use the loo as soon as possible, but, as she was under two at the time, it didn't seem to be a remote possibility. Both the boys were potty-trained by the age of two, Ben at eighteen months, and now my goal was to teach Alice the same, albeit later on in her timeline.

We – the tutors, or mostly Charlotte and I – turned this new loo experience into a game for Alice. She always had loose bowels, and rarely, if ever, did I open her nappy to find a 'well-formed stool'. Often her precious little bottom was scarred with rashes and red marks, even though I used up tubes and tubes of nappy cream trying to protect it. I realise this isn't a particularly pleasant topic to mention, and at the time I usually forgot about it until I inhaled the telltale smell of diarrhoea before opening up yet another foul-smelling nappy. Sometimes it wouldn't be apparent until I saw the wet brown liquid seeping through her nappy and wetting her trousers, now stained with the remains of undigested breakfast and lunch.

It was now time to potty-train her, except it was easier to teach her to sit on the toilet with an inset child's seat. Much neater and with less residual mess. We made up songs that were meant to encourage her to hold 'it' in until she was sitting on the loo, if indeed she could balance on the seat. If this worked, then there would be no more smelly, leaky, objectionable nappies.

We had to time this perfectly, and Charlotte and I thought the best option was to strike just after Alice had had her lunch. So this was when we headed for the toilet. It mostly seemed to work, and, happily, she never fell off the seat. In any event, there was always someone close by to keep hold of her, while also holding their breath. This seems funny in retrospect, but was not quite so amusing at the time. Singing cheerful songs (beginning with ridiculous and pathetic lyrics like *Pee-pee on the loo*), with beaming smiles on our faces, and staggering as quickly as possible to the toilet, while also trying not to breathe, was an achievement in itself.

To be fair, the toilet visits worked most of the time, and when they did, Charlotte and I would look at each other and scream with delight, "Well done, Alice. Well done..." Words which cunningly concealed a mutual sigh of relief.

20

Diets Tried

Since we'd been in Bath, I'd started looking into diet and vitamin supplements in earnest, as well as any other protocols that might be helpful. I started going to see a well-respected naturopath in Wiltshire, and, after we had both had blood tests as well as urine and faecal samples analysed, under guidance, we used vitamins and minerals to try to balance Alice's system and keep mine in check. Alice was a little over three-and-a-half, and we were still on the road to nowhere in terms of a specific prognosis.

In keeping with my inquisitive nature, I had been looking into somewhat random alternatives to help Alice develop mentally. I'd discovered a system involving classical music that is meant to aid your brain to make connections and develop. The idea is that you listen to a piece of music on specially designed headphones for a certain amount of sessions over a period of weeks. The individual listener will first subconsciously familiarise themselves with all the instruments and their distinctive sounds in the piece. The music alternates between the left ear and the right, as well as in the directional position of the sound, i.e. sounding as if it is coming at you from the front or from behind.

After having listened to this piece once a day for a few weeks, you then listen to the same piece of music for the same period, but it is now missing one of the musical elements. In the following sessions, the music is gradually pared back until it has nothing more than a few instruments. Over time, your brain is meant to fill in the gaps, thereby exercising it. We had a small folder in which to record the sessions that had been completed, the time spent doing them and any noticeable changes in the student.

I remember one of Alice's tutors, Rosie, doing this vigilantly with Alice, and I also remember her trying it for herself. In the end, she stopped as it was making her feel giddy and sick! Alice seemed to enjoy it, though, and we used it as often as we could.

Every week Rosie would cycle up the hill that led to our house. She was phenomenally competent and a joy to have around, although she sometimes questioned my approaches to Alice's care – for example, the copious vitamins with which I supplemented her diet. I had started her on these based strictly on a myriad of blood tests done by a biomedical doctor and overseen by a nutritionist.

Rosie was always truthful and straightforward, but, even though at times we were at loggerheads regarding the vitamin issue, it never affected her devotion. You can buy vitamins, but you can't buy that measure of dedication.

When Rosie's time was finished, Anna took her place, but suddenly we didn't have much time left. Anna was extremely diligent and only too happy to fill in where anything was needed. Even turning her hand to cooking our gluten free sausages. She always did everything with her whole heart, and I was very grateful that I could trust her with the unglamorous side of life with Alice, as well as the more demanding things like her ABA!

I started Alice on various diets, beginning with a gluten-free one, which I also imposed on myself. I then tried a milk-free diet, which sadly meant no more ice cream, cream or, my favourite, butter! I had already randomly tried both of these diets in my early twenties when I was first diagnosed with MS; they had seemed to work as my vision and balance had returned to normal. These are relatively easy diets; especially now there are so many alternatives to dairy and gluten.

Then I tried a complex carbohydrate diet (CCD) for Alice, which meant only eating complex carbs. This was definitely harder and more involved; it needed much more research and diligence in cooking and in the preparation of her meals. At home I was pretty much one hundred per cent successful, but it was hard if we ate out, and even harder if we were at a friend's or my in-laws' house, although all the friends and relatives we visited were always very accommodating and only too happy to cater for our fiddly and frequently changing diet peculiarities. Anthony and Anne in particular never described the diet fads I organised for Alice as a strain, and I was very grateful that, if they found it difficult, they never complained. From a selfish point of view, I think this was possibly the reason why I stayed as well as I did when Alice was alive.

Maybe it helped her too, though I will never know. Ultimately, none of these regimes made any substantial difference to Alice, and it's hard to say whether it was worth the pain and anguish for us.

21

A Walking Girl

At Valley View Barn, there were good times too. I had made Alice a massive so-called 'playpen' area in the largest room downstairs, our sitting room. This essential safety area was constructed from items of furniture which were already mostly in place. A soft sofa, a footstool, a comfortable chair and a two-seater piano stool were organised around the television. I would place these earnestly, making sure there was no danger for her. It meant she had an area that was safe and secure as the piano stool was a big oblong one that she would never have been able to climb over. Alice spent her time in this area crawling around and shuffling from one activity to another, pulling herself up into a standing position and then sometimes flinging herself, with a grin, towards anyone who might be sitting on one of the sofas and burying her smiling face in their lap.

If I had to go and cook, or put on a wash, I would place toys and activities on the various cushioned surfaces for her to explore. I'd bought a colourful plastic square, which, when turned over, played a selection of the introductions to six different Mozart concertos. As Alice played with this, the concertos went on indefinitely, and if you believed the blurb on the box, her intellectual abilities were stretched way beyond our wildest expectations. I wonder what Mozart would have thought. Perhaps, in a plastic sort of way, he might have loved it.

When Alice was four months shy of four, she walked. It was the first week of May 2010, and I was in the kitchen preparing supper while Matthew was playing in a room nearby. I heard a noise, and as I turned around, I saw Alice walking in the kitchen alone. I couldn't believe it. There, right there before me, was a larger-than-life Alice, standing nonchalantly unaided and examining the fridge magnets.

She gave me an enormous grin, and I screamed for Matthew to come into the kitchen. He rushed in, and we stood together, side by side, both in a state of shock. I had never seen Alice walk on her own before – not even a little step to reach something. She still had no sense of danger or fear of anything. I never expected her to appear unannounced in the kitchen. I suddenly saw hazards everywhere. I had never imagined that she'd ever be capable of walking on her own, so I flew around the worktops, removing anything that might prove dangerous. I suddenly had to look out for everything; knives, forks, breakable plates, glasses, heavy objects that might land on one of her naked feet.

When we thought about it later, we guessed that she must have moved some piece of the furniture that made up her 'playpen'. Although, it was probably more likely that she had climbed over the soft footstool to make her break for freedom, as there was no evidence of anything having been disturbed. This might also explain her cheeky grin when I caught her eye as she glanced at me while exploring the large magnetic letters stuck to the fridge. I was completely mystified as to how she had compromised her safety den! But mostly I was thrilled that it had happened and she had walked; something I'd never dared hope for.

A couple of days later Matthew asked me if he could capture her walking on video, so, while I took the photos, he took a video on his Nintendo. At one point, Alice walked towards me, grinning and shutting her eyes, and Matthew calmly captured this monumental achievement on film.

As Alice grew in confidence, she would reject my hand when I tried to help her walk, and sometimes she'd even correct our direction, setting her face purposefully towards the route she wanted to take. In fact, from early on, she was reluctant to hold anyone's hand to help her. She never held a hand for comfort, and only when she was dying in hospital did she voluntarily reach out her hand to hold mine or David's. When walking, her actions didn't ever seem disobedient, just determined.

Despite the unexpected shock, no one can imagine the joy and excitement of the moment that day when I, Matthew, and then Ben and David, saw Alice walking alone, as if it were the most natural thing in the world. The hard work done by her and Sarah, her physio, and my painful memories, were now blotted out and forgotten with a welcome cheer of accomplishment and relief.

Long before we were in the last chapter of Alice's life, we lived in the frustrating 'nearlies'. Each milestone was a nearly achieved goal. Alice was nearly eating by herself, nearly toilet-trained, nearly pointing to things, nearly asking for food or a drink. Alice was nearly walking by herself. These nearlies never became actuals; that is, all except for her walking – which shone so brightly as an actual that it distracted me for some time from the frustration of the long road of nearlies still ahead.

Meanwhile, I was always looking for an answer to Alice's 'problems'. When I first arrived in Bath, that search was very much at the forefront of my mind. I thought that the experts there would be better than the experts in little old Rutland. In fact, Alice's carers in Rutland were one hundred per cent better than those in Bath, aside from the team at BOP and Three Ways. Her individual carers in Rutland had been incredible. Having experienced our unbelievable occupational therapist, with her room full of wondrous tools designed to awaken Alice's potential, I was now faced with one whose only therapy was breathing on Alice's hands. He was a nice man, but his blowing treatment, and on one occasion tapping her hand and then her feet, were deeply inadequate.

We tried working with a music therapist, which we hadn't had in Rutland. He was caring and loving towards Alice, and had many instruments, all of which he played, and he encouraged Alice to join in and pluck a guitar string when there was a gap in the music, or bang the drum he was playing in time to the beat. She was never able to 'join in', but she always enjoyed her time with him and revelled in his music. We had become a little stuck on various nursery rhymes, but as far as I could tell, they only became boring to her adult friends and me! Alice's eyes sparkled with happiness during all these sessions. She made anyone who was around her feel happy, while we were – ironically – trying to do the same for her.

22

Babington and Epilepsy

The first time I remember an epileptic episode being mentioned in connection with Alice – as opposed to a vague possible side effect that might be expected for any child with her difficulties – was when David and I went away for a rare minibreak.

We'd first stayed at Babington House just after I'd had Ben, ten years before we moved to Bath. We were young(ish) and carefree when we discovered this beautiful and somewhat decadent hotel, and now that were living in Bath, we were only a thirty-minute drive away. It was a rare, secret extravagance that we indulged ourselves in when we felt the need to be spoiled a little – providing that the money gods had been smiling on us. The staff were relaxed and friendly, and the drinks and food delicious. We both felt at home inside its friendly, old, shabby chic walls.

During this particular break, Alice, who was now four, was settling into our new home and her new school. We'd left her and the boys in the capable hands of my dear friend and stand-in mother and grandmother, Kay, as well as Rosie, one of Alice's tutors. We'd woken up on our first morning in Babington after a blissful night's sleep, then eaten breakfast like a king and queen, knowing the washing-up was going to be done somewhere else by someone else.

Unexpectedly, my phone rang. It was Rosie, telling me that she thought Alice had just had an epileptic seizure. "She is fine and safe now," she said. "I just wanted to let you know."

Until this point, at home there had never been any mention of epilepsy. We had never mentioned the conversation we'd had about this with Professor Clayton at Great Ormond Street Hospital to anyone. So I was in blissful ignorance of what was happening at home, savouring our precious two-day break at our favourite hotel; enjoying the fantasy of being young and carefree again, even if it was make-believe and only for a few hours.

And it was just a few hours, because the frosty bubble of reality burst all over us as soon as I took that phone call.

We packed up, paid the painfully large bill, found our car, barely talking or able to think straight. All the time, I reasoned to myself that the word 'seizure' could mean anything. Rosie might have been wrong in her assessment.

And surely we would have noticed if Alice was having fits – if indeed she was. No doubt, David was having similar misgivings as we drove home in silence.

When we arrived back at base less than hour or so later, Alice seemed the same as ever; in fact, we didn't notice anything like a fit until a good few months later. For the rest of her life, these fits remained a mystery. Alice was never diagnosed as epileptic, and yet her seizures were exactly like epileptic fits. Ever the enigma, but always our Alice.

I can't remember the first obvious 'fit'. It was probably a blinking one, during which Alice would blink rapidly, over and over again, but even this was explicable at the time. It could have been the result of a gust of wind from an open window, or one of our overenthusiastic dogs' wagging tails softly brushing her face, or even one of Alice's long eyelashes irritating her. Only months later, when her fitting was out of control in hospital, could I see what had probably always been happening right before me.

The first 'event' was possibly a drooling fit. I don't think I ever genuinely thought this unusual symptom through. Looking back, this all seems so sad, and I realise now just how clueless we all were. Not only us, but the doctors as well; every time Alice had a test for epilepsy, nothing showed up on the EEG scans.

23

Cornwall

Although there were hard times, there was also so much laughter and happiness in our lives with Alice. One of our real joys, especially when Alice could walk on her own, was the time we spent in Cornwall. She would walk and smile and walk and grin and walk until there was hardly any walking left to do. She didn't talk as such, but made gleeful noises as if to accompany the squawking gulls. Her face would shine; it was as if she was giggling, which is why I think so many still believe that she did laugh and giggle out loud. She'd walk for hours without any sense of danger and seemed oblivious to any discomfort she might be causing her delicate feet.

We often drove the interminable route to Cornwall, Alice sitting in her oversized baby's car seat. During the journey, I'd frequently turn round and check that all was well. If Ben was beside Alice and she was awake, I could be sure he'd willingly reassure her, which she sometimes needed on such a long journey. He would voluntarily take hold of her hand and give her a reassuring grin. If she became at all upset or frustrated, I knew he'd be the one to calm the storm. Other times Matthew might be sitting by her side, and I would ask him to entertain her. He was equally adept at making Alice forget the length of the journey ahead.

The two boys taught me so much during the years Alice was with us. Their patience and acceptance were astonishing. Neither would argue or sulk if I asked them to turn over the TV or turn off their DVD right in the middle so that Alice could watch something that only interested her. They were still at the stage of *Thomas the Tank Engine* and perhaps *Thunderbirds*, but they definitely would not have chosen Mr Tumble. Mr Tumble's Makaton signing, singing and colourful outfits were a delight to Alice and a vital learning tool for us, but they didn't particularly appeal to the boys. Neither of them ever complained, and I'm in awe of the patience they showed.

I had also noticed that Alice's father calmed her and gave her a deep sense of peace that no one else was able to do. There were a few occasions when nothing would bring Alice to a place of rest like spending time with David. There were times I would hear that she was unable to sleep, and I would go into her room to try to settle her. On some of those occasions, I wasn't able to do anything for her, and then I would go back to our bedroom opposite to ask David to go and talk to her, which he would faithfully do. He would pick her up, and hold her while she snuggled her head deep into his neck and shoulder. Miraculously, any sign of unhappiness or discomfort she had been displaying was instantly forgotten. She would utter gentle, calming murmurs, as if under her breath. Then I would wonder why it had taken me so long to ask David. He had the authority and certainty of trustworthiness and dependability that she craved and needed.

The summer before Alice died we had our happiest and best holiday in England. Even the car journey was different from those of previous years, when we had always seemed to end up trapped in aggravating traffic jams, and the boys would invariably bicker. David would be fractious and exhausted, and I'd be stressed and worn out. Only Alice, who usually slept for a good part of the journey, seemed mostly content with life. As the school year had drawn to a close in June 2011, everyone seemed settled and happy, and this continued into August when we drove to Trebetherick for our summer holiday.

That year we stayed in a rented house close to the beach, near enough for us to be able to walk back after a morning on the sand. This meant we could eat, reapply sun cream, change into or out of swimming costumes, collect another ball or bat, or change Alice. The car was parked in the drive and hardly used. The weather was also unusually warm and sunny for England.

Looking back, after Alice died, we appreciated this

holiday all the more. They were magnificent days, when Alice enjoyed walking with David and let him dress her in her damp and sandy wetsuit so that she could go with him into the sea. We saw Chris and Adelle and their son, Sam, who made us all laugh. Sam, a friend of his, and our younger boys enjoyed building a magnificent sandcastle, and laughed hilariously about nothing in particular. Adelle walked with Alice up to the sea and went right up to the noisily breaking waves together with Naomi, who was spending the summer holiday helping us. My father also came on this holiday and braved the waves with his granddaughter; he held Alice above the wild water as she splashed her legs in the foam with delight. She loved being with him and found great joy in feeling safe in his strong hands. This was a long, beautiful and carefree time.

It was only at the very end of the holiday that I began to notice that Alice's seizures, which had started about a year before, were getting worse and were no longer adequately controlled by her latest medication. Although I was aware that things were deteriorating, I chose to look away from any problem as there was nothing I could do about it while we were miles away from home on holiday.

24

Epilepsy, and Yet Not

As soon as we got back to Bath, I addressed the fitting issue and began hounding the doctors. As time went on and things with Alice deteriorated fairly rapidly, I frequently had to call 999 as her seizures became progressively longer and more and more frightening.

When the ambulance arrived, its siren piercing the sleepy outskirts of Bath, the paramedics would rush into the house in a flurry of noisy activity and then whisk away our little girl, and one of us, to the hospital.

The unmistakable sound of ambulance sirens rapidly became the anthem to this new stage of Alice's all-too-short life. Once I remember sitting in the back of the rescue vehicle and holding Alice tenderly and whispering sweet everythings into her ear. As we pulled into the centre of the city, close to the A&E at the Royal United Hospital, in the background I could make out the echo of a siren, and I remember asking the paramedics where the ambulance was that I could hear, but couldn't see. They replied that I was sitting in it. A chill of reality hit me; a cold mixture of pain and fear that didn't leave me until long after she went.

As time went on, and I realised how serious everything was getting, I hoped to get Alice admitted to hospital so that she could be looked after, watched and maybe given some long-term treatment. During a seizure we would sometimes rush Alice to hospital when there were two of us, or, if I was alone, I'd have to take her on my own. The fits got worse and worse, and, before she was finally admitted to hospital, more and more frequent. Subtly, little by little, they became hideously exaggerated. If we were both at home, one of us would talk to the boys, calm them and try to explain what was happening to their sister. If the television was on, we'd ask them to turn it off. One of us would call the ambulance; then we'd hold our breath in anticipation of hearing the sirens getting closer and closer, while also trying to place Alice into a safe position and reassure her as much as we could. The unmistakable flashing blue lights would illuminate our kitchen, and the paramedics would sweep in and either bundle Alice out and into the waiting ambulance, or, if the seizure was over and she'd fallen asleep, they would assess her and discuss the possible implications of her staying at home with us or alternatively going to hospital.

We never had to wait long for an ambulance, but by the time the now-familiar team arrived, more often than not, the fit would have passed and Alice would be asleep from exhaustion.

"It's OK; you're doing so well. We're so sorry, darling. Well done, dearest Alice." Our futile words were left languishing on the carpet to gather dust as the medics silently stepped over them and vanished quickly out of the open door.

When we realised that Alice had severe epilepsy (though it's hard to call it that because her scans were clear, so I'll have to call them undefined seizures), we knew that we were incapable of caring for her. We had been waiting for the doctor to suggest bringing Alice into hospital so that she could stay and be assessed. To no avail.

So on Boxing Day 2011, we decided to take her to A&E, hoping that she would be admitted. She was mid-seizure and had had a terrible morning, fitting frequently. We had to take the boys as well as Alice, to the hospital.

The room we sped into was overflowing with people with broken bones, cut hands, blood flowing from various places, bloodied tissues pressed to wounds. Some people were drunk or had head injuries, or both. There was trauma and noise everywhere; the place was pandemonium. We were seen after a wait of a couple of hours, by which time Alice was fast asleep and there was nothing to report. As we got to the front of the queue, we knew that we were going to be sent home again, having wasted what felt like days. All of us waited patiently, only too aware of the likely lack of a favourable outcome. Both Ben and Matthew, yet again, displayed unusual maturity and kindness to David and me by not interrupting Alice and refrained from screaming for our attention.

We'd previously had frequent tests to ascertain whether Alice had epilepsy or not. During the thirty to sixty minutes of an EEG test, electrodes made of small metal discs with thin wires attached were pasted onto Alice's scalp with a sticky, odourless, clear glue-type substance. These electrodes were used to detect abnormalities or unusual electrical activity in her brainwaves. This process could take anywhere between three and five hours out of our day. I'd watched the various nurses during the frequent tests, laboriously gluing these hard, round, tiny nodules onto the skin under Alice's beautiful hair, all in very exact locations. The currents running from one electronic pad to another had revealed nothing to indicate an epileptic seizure. We had a final EEG in the RUH, which, even though Alice was mid-fit during the recording, showed conclusively that there was no traditional epileptic anything.

After the tests, once we had returned home, I would wash away the sticky muck that had been used to glue the test nodules to her head, while simultaneously trying to wash away the memory of the day. I knew I had to wait for the clinical neurophysiologist's assessment of the scan, and I would often tearfully wonder how, so far, nothing on earth had been found. Alice was undoubtedly getting worse, and her symptoms were being played down or ignored by the medics. We were desperate for help, which we weren't getting. I sent recording after recording of the seizures she was now having to the neurologist in charge of her case in Bath, but these graphic episodes were wholly ignored. This is possibly explicable, given that the tests she had refuted any epileptic activity. The only alternative reason given for her behaviour was reflux. Reflux! We had been trying and trying to get a referral, but now the doctors agreed with one another. They were explaining her symptoms as being the result of a digestive issue! To say I found this difficult to understand is a gross understatement. I couldn't marry this explanation with the shocking physical episodes that Alice was now experiencing.

So, despite sending a deluge of videos to the paediatrician in Bath, I got nowhere. In truth, I don't think the doctor watched a single one. In fairness to him, I'm sure he had a lot going on in his busy working life and if an EEG test said nothing, then, quite understandably, to him that meant nothing could be done.

Alice had 'dropping' (atonic) fits, during which she would become listless and then fall to the ground. She had 'proper' (grand mal) seizures, where she groaned and shook violently, and her eyes rolled in their sockets. During these times she was inconsolable and never seemed aware of anyone or anything except whatever it was that was torturing her. She had also started having groaning episodes in which she clearly (at least to me and those who were nearby) had no control over her body, let alone her voice. I described these fits but, despite the gruesome video evidence, the doctor in charge still didn't feel Alice needed to be observed or cared for in hospital. I listened to the young doctor to whom I'd sent all the video clips, and was advised to take her off all her epilepsy medications. It was so confusing; we could all see seizures of some kind, some of which were very dramatic, and then she was given an 'all-clear'. I wasn't clear what I should do!

I was beginning to feel properly scared. I felt like a child myself, unable to cope. I needed someone else, outside of my immediate world, to come and tell me what was wrong and then, preferably, fix it.

I silently questioned, *Should I bow to this young doctor; the one I am sending copious video recordings to? Should I really accept that I'm just a crazy mother who's misreading her daughter's reflux symptoms?* I couldn't stay quiet, especially after all the evidence I'd seen myself of these frightening episodes.

Nothing could have prepared us for the oncoming tsunami of suffering that Alice endured. The groans that emanated from her little body, her shortness of breath, and the way her body stiffened whenever she had one of these 'whatever-they-were things'. The 'things' which we were no longer allowed to call epilepsy. Much later, when Alice was in the RUH, she would groan and sometimes scream and then gasp for breath. Her whole body would harden and inflate, her back bending towards the ceiling.

Whenever she was suffering one of these episodes, the expression on her face was agonising.

On numerous occasions, she was rushed to hospital in an ambulance, and yet again we were told that her episodes were not the result of any medical seizure. My unspoken questions thundered in my head: *So, what are they? What on earth is going on?* These are questions that will no doubt always remain unanswered.

I still don't know where I got the idea that someone, somewhere, probably dressed in a white coat, would have all the answers. I don't know why I felt that there had to be an explanation. Possibly it came from an understandable but misguided expectation that Alice would remain with us forever on this earth and that there was someone out there who could guarantee that this would happen.

I might have questioned my faith at this time, but I never did. Fortunately, neither did David. The obvious question that echoed in my head was that, if God claimed Alice as belonging to Him, why did she have to suffer such intolerable pain? I have no answer to that, not even a trite one. My consolation is that we were reliably told that during a seizure the sufferer will have no memory of the event or even having suffered.

25

Two Hospitals in the South-West

Neither David nor I can remember precisely how Alice ended up in the Royal United Hospital (RUH), Bath, as an inpatient. We think it was because she was in mid-fit when we took her to A&E and the doctors had no choice but to keep her in. It was just after Christmas, when Alice was five. For David and me, this was a huge relief.

The RUH was our local hospital, and when Alice was first admitted, she shared a room with five other children. The other kids came and went, and we stayed. There was no change for the better, no stability. Alice was put on various medications to try to control her seizures, but again, probably because her condition was not classic epilepsy, the drugs didn't do very much, and although they seemed to work for a while, possibly her system was getting used to the treatment too. We took it in turns to sleep over, hunched up in the chair at the end or by the side of her bed, trying to meld into the shape of the hard plastic seat, fruitlessly grabbing a few seconds of inadequate sleep with only a thin hospital blanket for warmth. David was working flat out at this time, still trying to balance our financial books. He would usually stay at the hospital on a Friday or Saturday night and sometimes both, and either he or I would go home to look after the boys. It was a case of divide and conquer.

During this time, Charlie and Sheena came to our rescue. When they'd been living in Malawi, they'd met a couple who had subsequently moved to Bath. When they'd come over to visit they had introduced us to them, and when Sheena heard about what we were going through she called their friends from Africa and asked them to look out for us. I believe her actual words were, "Please will you be us both to David and Joanna?"

Rick and Cathy were as good as her word and conveniently they lived within a few minutes of the RUH, less than a mile away. They were thoughtful and generous. Early on, while we were still in the RUH, they brought us home-cooked, gluten-free pasta dishes and glasses of chilled white wine. By then we were longing to get to Bristol Royal Hospital for Children, where we knew there was an exceptional paediatric team who specialised in neurology. We prayed that they might know more about the complex conditions in 'children like Alice'.

It subsequently occurred to me that I probably should have stopped the epilepsy medicine, especially since Alice was not classed as having epilepsy. But in her early days of having fits, the drugs had worked, so I didn't dare stop them. I had to believe that the doctors knew more than I did, though by their own admission they were holding hands with us in the dark. How does one ever decide to give up? I just don't know. As I've already said, I don't seem to have the 'giving up' gene in my DNA.

The month we were stationed (I'm tempted to say 'imprisoned') in the RUH was not a happy time. None of the medications seemed to be working. With the occasional help of Charlotte and David, I tried to provide twenty-four-hour care for Alice, as well as coping in the afternoons and evenings with all the boys' needs. The RUH turned out to be an awful experience, in the midst of many other intolerable and inexplicable medical things in my life at that time.

One of the issues for me was the overall cleanliness of the ward. The floor was 'cleaned' using a thoroughly inadequate, dark grey mop which was shunted around the floor as if it was fast asleep. I certainly think the operator was. There were many smelly, unemptied bins which were probably breeding new life forms, and the gooey dirt skulking around the legs of the beds and the chairs did not help the overall ambience of the place. Kay, who was never far from my side, and I both caught horrid hospital bugs.

We were waiting for the very same doctor who had failed to take any interest in my videos of Alice's fits to refer us to the Bristol Children's Hospital and discharge us from his care in Bath. Every day dragged interminably. Looking back, I'm not sure how I coped with this. Apart from Rick and Cathy, I didn't know anyone who could help me out. We'd only been in Bath for a little over two years, and sadly, the few people I did know had their own busy lives and their own busy children to look after.

We still had Charlotte manning the fort, and I think she did most of the school pickups. It was a very peculiar time, which is thankfully now just a hazy memory. It was only after Alice died that meals were dropped on our doorstep by thoughtful friends, which was ironic, since by then I had plenty of time. Time to think and to shop, and hours to cook and struggle through as best I could. I had many, many days to waste my grieving time away.

After a month in the RUH, a bed became available in the Bristol Children's Hospital, and we were moved on. Alice went in an ambulance, and I sat with her while David followed in the car. I saw this as the answer. The neurology team would surely be able to find out what was wrong with our daughter, and then her condition would be treated, and we'd finally be able to return home, relieved and happy. It was inconceivable to me that this would not be the case. I was ready to hand over most of Alice's care to these professionals, and then I could relax, knowing she was in the best hands that would give us all the answers. I genuinely always thanked God for the dedication of the nurses and doctors, and their unparalleled skills and devotion.

When we finally arrived at the Bristol Children's Hospital and explored the ward, we were shown to the room where Alice would be staying with three others. While we were waiting for a nurse in the communal area outside the rooms, Alice astutely decided to empty the entire contents of her post-lunch stomach all over her front, the pushchair and the newly disinfected floor. I shouted for help, and all the available nurses came bustling over. Miraculously, they cleared everything up. Bliss! I didn't have to lift a finger or touch a sponge. This also meant a change of plan, and Alice was given a private room, with an en-suite bathroom. More bliss! Goodness knows what all this luxury cost the NHS, especially as we ended up staying in this room for the next four months.

We now needed to find someone to sit with Alice overnight. I couldn't carry on doing five or six nights a week, and now I was much further away from our home and the boys' school in Bath. On a clear run, it would take a little over forty-five minutes door to door to get to the Bristol Children's Hospital as opposed to half an hour to the RUH in Bath. I would be travelling during rush hour every day, so the time taken could in fact be at least double this. Being with Alice during the night also meant carefully writing down the number and types of seizures she was having, while buzzing the nurses so they could administer medication to stop her going into 'status'. This is a term used to describe a fit which has become unstoppable and could quite possibly prove fatal.

I was trying to do all this while at the same time carrying out all my other duties as a mother: laundry, bed-making, cooking, reading practice, also revision and homework. Apart from this, I still tried to provide some fun for the boys; some time to catch up, as well as to provide the comfort and love that they, as eight- and ten-year-old children, still needed. I tried to do all of this with as much patience and love as was humanly possible. I can't say I was always successful, but I did the best I could. I haven't mentioned my wifely duties, but I'm afraid most of the time David and I were like the proverbial ships passing in the night, waving hello and blowing an occasional kiss across the hospital floor. We found the most efficient communication came from holding each other's gaze with the knowledge that comes from searching one another's souls and wordlessly conveying what we wanted but were unable to say.

I managed to organise a rota for the night-time, which was now going to be covered individually by a few of Alice's carers. Alice had changed so much in the five weeks or so since she'd last been at home, so that most of those who knew her would have no idea what her new 'normal' behaviour was. I made a list of all the different types of fits, episodes, seizures or whatever these physical manifestations were, so that everyone involved in her care would be able to recognise what was now normal for her and what wasn't. Under my instructions, they all kept notes of their observations, which I, in turn, kept in a file so that I could assess the efficacy of the medication she was taking. It meant I could also see more clearly if she was improving or not. Below is the list I gave her carers of her most recent symptoms:

1. Drop fits (head and torso suddenly collapsing).
2. Blinking fits (mild to severe blinking, from fast to uncontrollable).
3. Absences (hard to spot when very mild, but when they are longer she doesn't react to the clicking of fingers or waving of a hand in front of her eyes).
4. Drooling (nearly always accompanies all fits; salivation can be mild dribbling to liquid pouring out of her mouth as if from a tap).
5. Clonic (usually only her head, where it appears she is straining to look up and her neck is stiff and pushed back. Her mouth usually distorts and her breathing is irregular; plus she appears distressed).
6. Tonic (one or both arms are extended forward or are flung up in the air and go stiff and shake).
7. Clonic/tonic (combining the two above fits. Alice has had a few clonic/tonic fits over the last few months. So far they appear very mild and are usually short-lived).
8. Less frequent fits that she seems to have stopped having: groaning/screaming/heart palpitations (she has been on a heart monitor – and at one point, also an oxygen monitor).
9. Anything else that is not normal for her, please write up!

I stuck this list onto the inside front cover of my hospital folder. I had decorated the cover with stickers which I'd accumulated over the years of homeschooling. I'd found flower nymphs holding out flowers and balloons, which

I followed with a trail of golden stars. I added a 'WELL DONE' sticker and surrounded it with love hearts and kisses, hoping, ridiculously, that this would be a subliminal message of my overwhelming pride in Alice. I wanted anything colourful to be stuck onto the file – anything that might belie the pain recorded inside it. I had printed stacks of paper, headed with the date and time, and spaces that were to be filled in during the hours spent with Alice. Spaces for the type and duration of her seizures, as well as the medication that was administered to her. By the end, she was having over a hundred convulsions per day.

It was, if I'm frighteningly honest, a total waste of time. Perhaps in another story, one in which she had lived and we had found a cure, it might not have been. I say this now, again, with the twenty-twenty wisdom of hindsight.

Eventually, many of the overnight spells were done by Juliet or Hazel, or sometimes by Charlotte. Hazel was an old friend of Charlotte's, and she always arrived at the hospital looking fabulous. Carefully made-up and stylishly dressed, she loved Alice, and I loved the care she lavished on her. Amongst other things, Hazel is a talented photographer, and early on she'd given me a square canvas print with a photograph of Alice resting on a pink, heart-shaped cushion on her hospital bed. I still sleep with this cushion on our bed, and I have the picture of Alice that Hazel gave us, on the wall facing us.

The cushion under Alice's head, which lies with me now, has letters in bold pink velvet, spelling out the word 'Love', on a cream heart which is superimposed onto the cushion. This is probably the size of a baby pillow, and was given to Alice very early on in her hospital stay by my god-daughter, Shanti, who at the time was nearly thirteen. Shanti had been with us in Cape Town when Alice was only one and is Charlie and Sheena's eldest daughter. The design of the cushion was not something I would have picked out, but it's the sort of thing teenagers love, and I was grateful for this gift to Alice. It turned out to be invaluable in helping to prop Alice's head up and give her the physical support she needed when she was sitting in bed. It also looked cheerful and comforting against her crisp white hospital sheets. This small gift was very special to me at the time, and recently when Shanti was staying with us I told her how much it meant to me and just how grateful I was then, and still am. She had forgotten all about it and was touched when she realised how important it had been. She is now twenty-one, and she laughed generously when I described it as 'naff'!

In the photograph Hazel gave us, Alice looks happy and peaceful, with an enigmatic smile, not dissimilar to the smile on the face of the *Mona Lisa*. The picture isn't as perplexing as Da Vinci's classic painting, particularly because Alice has a plastic feeding tube protruding from her nose.

Soon after Hazel gave me the print of Alice on this cushion, I started to record our time together at the hospital photographically. As a keen (very) amateur photographer, I had kept my camera hidden away since we'd been in hospital. It was only when I received Hazel's print that I decided to take photos, and now I have a pictorial record of this awful time. I had been convinced that this was only a stage in Alice's life, and I felt it was not a time I'd want to remember. However, when Hazel gave me her photo, I realised that I did want to record our time together as a family even time spent during those terrifying months.

They were curious days spent together, snuggled on her bed, chatting and laughing, making things as 'ordinary' as possible. I started to take lots of photos, as I had done throughout our lives together. Many of these I have to skim through now, as some are just too distressing for me to see. It's a shame that my fruit-based computer and phone decide to run 'memories' of some of these events, once even labelling the few days before she died, along with her funeral, with the cheerful title *Growing Up*. Someone with a more delicate disposition than mine might object verbally to this gross intrusion. Either that or roll over, down the pills and shut their eyes.

I have decided I might have to put all these photos, and the videos I sent to the neurologist of Alice fitting, on a memory stick that I can hide somewhere. That way, I'll never have to look at Alice when she was so sick, ever again.

It's a shame I can't lock the memories away as easily.

I couldn't be more grateful that I knew then, and even more so now, that this was not the end of Alice's life. On this earth, yes, it was near the end, but eternally, for all of us, I don't remotely believe that this is all there is.

26

Paintings on a Wall

Days drifted into weeks, which disappeared seamlessly into months. The new norm was trying to get into Bristol before the rush hour. A journey that on a clear run should take about forty-five minutes could become an horrific one-and-a-half-hour hell of bumper-to-bumper, fuel-belching traffic jam. All I wanted to do was spend every nanosecond with Alice, and every second wasted could easily reduce me to tears.

Charlotte, whom I still see occasionally and, thanks to social media, still keep in touch with, was my home help and nanny. She was a little miracle worker, and she mostly kept our show on the road. Charlotte would often stay at home with the boys or at the hospital, and it was always a security blanket for me when I knew it was her turn to stay with Alice. She seemed to carry the weight of the world so lightly on her young shoulders. I also loved her hilarious stories of her carefree nights out and subsequent lost shoes, or, more often than not, just the one lost shoe! She recently reminded me of the many missing phones, wallets, glasses and sometimes entire handbags that accompanied her evening frivolities!

Sometimes a friend, who also had a child at the boys' school, would kindly pick Ben and Matthew up and drop them at school. Other times I had to do it. This involved a stressful amount of organisation. I had to walk the dogs before leaving, knowing I wasn't going to be at home for at least eight hours, hoping they would be able to do all their doggy business before I left. I would repeatedly chuck a ball down the hill that bordered our house in an attempt to exhaust our young Labrador as well as entertain our ageing Jack Russell. The latter dog I hoped wouldn't catch the scent of a rabbit or a pheasant and then disappear for hours. I'd call the dogs in, make sure they had their food, and then either shoot off to school with Ben and Matthew or wait until their lift arrived. I then sped, as legally as possible, into Bristol.

I was starving, but surviving on a diet high on adrenaline and emotional pain.

It hit me one morning. David was away, and I'd done everything that needed to be done – I'd got dressed and repeatedly woken the boys, scraping them out of bed. I'd fed them, helped make sure they had everything they might need for school – games shirts, homework projects, classroom necessities, reading books, pencil cases – and I still had to remember to pack up the kitchen sink! By this time, I'd also been outside, exercised the dogs and given them their food.

Then something inside me snapped.

Seemingly out of nowhere, I was hit with the full force of the unbearable emotional pain that I was trying to bury. I was in the kitchen when it happened. I had finished doing everything and was bending down to place the dogs' fresh water bowl on the floor. The boys, in their smart school uniforms, were waiting patiently beside me. My beautiful gift of a handbag was now heavy and cumbersome but hugely useful. I used this to carry everything in, including all the things I might need for the hospital and for Alice. This was balancing precariously on one of my shoulders. As I bent down, I could feel the bag very gradually slipping down my arm, and then, as if without warning, it suddenly crashed violently into the water bowl, sending the bowl and its contents flying into the air. The walls, floor, ceiling, kitchen cupboards and worktop were all dripping wet. It was the last straw. I doubled up and screamed – a scream which seemed to encompass all the fury, agony and exhaustion that I'd been holding in for so long.

The scream was so loud, and so long, that it was impossible to shield Ben and Matthew from what was happening to their mother. When I surfaced mentally and physically from my distressing outburst, I saw them both staring open-mouthed at me. I wiped my nose and brushed away my tears, and began to stammer out an apology, not only for my shocking explosion but for everything that they were now living. I quickly mopped up the worst of the water, filled the bowl again, checked that the dogs and, more importantly, my boys were OK, and we left for school.

I finally got onto the road to Bristol, the only road that I longed to be on, half an hour late, just in time to catch the rush-hour festival leading into the city. It was now time to lurch in the hiccupping line of barely moving traffic, knowing my boys were facing their day alone, hopefully not too freaked out by their mother's unexpected explosion.

Mostly I would listen to music as I drove to Bristol. A friend had made me a CD of many of my favourite songs, songs that spoke to my deepest insecurities and most dreaded fears, and songs which also spoke of my hope in God. Hope that He was with me through everything, that He would never let me go, and that He knew and understood my desperation. I would weep and weep as I drove, blinking furiously to keep my overflowing eyes focused on the oncoming traffic. Often I would cry out of exasperation, or, in the privacy of my car, moan quietly to myself at the hopelessness and fear I felt because Alice didn't seem to be getting any better. They were words and moans that overflowed from my sobbing, breaking heart. Perhaps these were the cries mentioned in the Bible:

> In the same way, the Spirit also helps us in our weakness, since we do not know

> how to pray as we should. But the Spirit Himself intercedes for us with groans too deep for words.
>
> Romans 8:26

Occasionally I would catch myself thinking subconsciously about driving into a wall, or through a barrier and over the bridge into the water beyond, and then it would all be over. This was a strange kind of fantasy. In reality, I would never have done anything like that, and it was never, ever a conscious thought. Possibly this horror show was a side effect of my buried grief, which, incidentally, kept showing up and playing on my internal video screen long after Alice had died. I would also often pray during these journeys, filling my car with my stumbling prayers, my way of talking intimately with my Lord and my comforter.

I usually parked opposite the Bristol Children's Hospital. As I left my car, my eyes would invariably be drawn to the wall above an empty shop immediately above where I'd parked. There was always a sketch in black paint, sometimes with 'typed' lettering. These pictures changed regularly and randomly. The sketches were arresting, thought-provoking, sometimes humorous or rude, and always moving. They would embolden or cheer my day. I might look up and see a line drawing of a girl floating ahead while holding on to a red heart-shaped helium balloon. She might be looking back over her shoulder with an unidentifiable smile. Sometimes they were merely irreverent and funny cartoons. I knew that Banksy lived in or near Bristol and always wondered if he could have done them, and I wish I'd taken photos of the different images. I have since looked up this shop on the internet, and this is somewhere he apparently uses. These drawings and sometimes paintings filled me up, lightened the start of my day and always made me smile. How the artist did them, I will probably never know, but this is a massive shout-out to him for feeding my emaciated heart when it most needed sustenance.

In hospital I spent my time sitting in Alice's bed with her and squinting at all the rubbish daytime programmes on her small TV. I decorated her room with colourful bunting and hung up some of the 'Get Well' cards we'd been sent around the room, trying to make it look as cheerful as possible. As often as I could, I would take her outside onto a small terrace which ran alongside the hospital rooms on our side of the ward. This passage had an overhanging landing above, which gave us a much-needed umbrella cover when it was drizzling. Leaving the claustrophobic ward, and going outside into the fresh air, gave me, and hopefully Alice, a welcome change of scenery.

Outside, along this terrace, there were toys and lots of colourful items to enjoy. There was a plastic toy kitchen with an oven and a play workbench for budding young builders, and there was also a giant Connect 4 game. Alice loved randomly fiddling and playing with the bright yellow Polo-shaped counters. I would often walk with her up and down the length of the terrace. I walked as many times as possible to try to keep her legs from losing their strength.

By then, I had a mental dictionary of words which I used when talking to her doctors, carers, or the nurses in the hospital – unusual words describing her physical disabilities. Words describing the different types of seizures she was having, as well as the reams and reams of drugs that she was trying, not to mention the words I needed to describe the side effects she was displaying. I have mostly forgotten these words and don't want to write about them anyway because of the memories they might evoke. At the time, I never thought I'd be able to forget any of them, but I have completely and utterly forgotten them all. I have files and files and boxes and boxes of information that I used to keep 'just in case'. I decided not to destroy any of these files or papers after Alice died because every little detail about her life was such an essential part of my own.

But now I look at it all, and I think I might be nearly ready to leave it all behind and burn the whole lot, just as I have completely suppressed my now-forgotten hospital words.

For the first few months at the hospital, there was no matron, and we seemed to have fallen through various gaps in the nursing care system. Usually, we would have been given a night nurse for Alice, but no one had been appointed. We hadn't counted on her having a nurse selected solely for her anyway, and so we'd arranged for one of us to be with her each night to make sure she felt safe. She might sleep, or, more likely, suffer any number of fits, but at least she would be with someone she knew, a comforting friend. Towards the end, we had run out of not only energy, but also money. By this time a matron had fortuitously been chosen for our department. We were promptly given a member of the nursing team to sit with Alice during the nights. It wasn't ideal, but by that time, there was no alternative.

There were only a few times at hospital that I can remember feeling joyful. One warm, sunny day at the end of May, shortly before Alice was diagnosed with pneumonia, I took her out of the hospital in her pushchair and onto the street outside. She loved watching all the buses and taxis and listening to the beep of the zebra crossing. Alice grinned, and I knew, in that moment, how happy she was. There was another time with Naomi, when we had been walking on the ward with Alice, and she had spontaneously burst out giggling. However, it wasn't long after this that she was unable to walk more than a few yards from her room. She was with me, a nurse and once again, Naomi, when I had to quickly sweep her up in my arms to take her back to her room after a dangerous 'dropping fit'. This was another gross nudge illustrating her deteriorating health.

When I was in the hospital looking after Alice on a daily, and sometimes nightly, basis, I took over some of her nursing care. I learnt to administer her drugs, which, to begin with, was nerve-racking. Alice was being fed via a nasogastric tube, which passed up her nose and down into her stomach. Usually, a child would have a gag reflex and would retch as it went in or was taken out, but Alice didn't react at all. Given that the tube was changed regularly, this was a welcome relief. This tube was used for her food as well as for most of her medications.

To check that the tube in her nose and running through into her stomach was working, I learnt how to draw some of the fluid in her stomach up and out of her nose to test it. I then had to squeeze out the dubious mixture onto a small tester strip to check the pH value. If the tube had moved from her stomach, it might mean that anything passed into it would go into her lungs, which, if they were filled with anything other than oxygen, would be catastrophic. Only when all the preliminaries had been checked was I free to either give her food or the drugs which usually stopped her fitting and sent her to sleep.

One of the other, more powerful anti-epileptic drugs given to Alice, paraldehyde, was so potent that, if it took too long to administer, it would melt the thick plastic tube that was needed to insert the drug into her rectum. Paraldehyde was a paste-like substance with an extremely smelly, lingering and unpleasant odour which hung in the air long after it was administered. I had to try to squeeze the noxious-smelling drug as quickly as possible into the plastic-straw-like tube first, then place this tube into Alice's bottom, before using a large plastic syringe to push the drugs into her body. I can't remember precisely what this process entailed, but I do remember that shortly before Alice died, she pushed my hand away, so that I and all the nurses in the room knew that she didn't want me to give her this drug any more. If the substance could melt the tube, goodness knows what it was doing to her precious insides. This was one of the very few times Alice ever indicated to me what she wanted, or, in this case, most certainly did not want.

The doctors had no plan. I had no idea where we were heading. All I had was a deep fear and a burning need for answers. I examined the words from the Bible that I felt had been given to me when I was in my twenties, some of which I had understood as references to my three children. I searched for anything that might give me a clue as to what was going on, specifically those that spoke about my 'offspring'. They provided little information or hope as I struggled to interpret them. I was terrified that Alice was dying. I checked the last few verses in the original Hebrew, the words which I guessed spoke of her: "Another will write with his hand, 'The LORD's', And name himself by the name of Israel". (Isaiah 44:5)

'Write with', I found in Hebrew can also be translated as 'To write, record or enrol.' (Hebrew: Kathab). Could this speak of the fact that David and I had named her and registered her birth?

Then I looked at what to 'name himself' means, (Hebrew: Kanah). This can also be translated as 'to be surnamed'. Might this refer to Alice's death, and then God giving her a new name in Heaven? My crazed, frantic, desperate mind was taking me anywhere and nowhere.

The fact that she would 'write with [her] hand, "The LORD's"' might be understood to mean that she never spoke with her voice, but only communicated very basically with her hand. Or was this a recognition of the mark on her ring finger? These irrational questions are destined to remain utterly unanswerable.

I was trying to find a reason for all that was happening in my life, and the illness that Alice was so clearly suffering from, but I wasn't given any clear answer in these words. I find knowing what is going to happen so much easier than being unsure. When I can see the future, I can make preparations and plan, however dreadful it looks. When I don't know, I feel desperately out of control and lost. Worse than that, during this horrendous time, every day I felt as if I was lost in a field of nettles, surrounded by hidden scorpions.

There was one incident that remains as real to me today as any experience I have ever had. I am not known for showing my emotions, particularly the difficult ones, to those around me. But one day, as I left Alice's room and shut the door behind me, I walked into the ward by the nurses' station, and lost my composure. I staggered to the lift, suddenly sobbing uncontrollably. When the nurses showed their concern and offered their help, I couldn't speak. Instead, I just shook my head and waved them away with a gesture that implied I was all right. I was trapped in the middle of my internal raging battleground; I was in a hurry to get to the boys' school to pick them up, while desperate not to be apart from my daughter.

As I staggered across the street and towards my parked car, a young, vibrant-looking couple, presumably university students, were walking past. They could see the distress I was in, and stopped in their tracks to repeatedly insist on helping me. But I didn't want their help, and I certainly didn't want to express what I was feeling, though my turmoil must have been relatively clear. All I wanted to do was shout and scream: *I've just had to leave my daughter in hospital, and she is dying, my daughter is dying… and I don't have a choice. I have to leave her…*

But how could I have spoken these words aloud? I felt they were real but I certainly didn't want to admit that I really thought she was dying. The words would have been a needless admission of defeat and desperate resignation. I didn't say anything. Instead, I carried on getting into my car, and as I carelessly fell into the driver's seat, I was hardly able to breathe, let alone shoot a backward glance to thank the kind young strangers for their concern.

The one good thing this showed me was that, despite the challenges I was facing – the fear of being the one responsible for Alice, together with the profound physical and emotional impact this little life was having on my own – I still never wanted to be without her. I didn't ever want to let her go. Even though I had always been confident that I would see her again one day, I wanted her to stay with me, in my life here.

27

Nearing the End

At this point, we probably only had a further six weeks in Bristol to get through, but life seemed to jog along as 'normal' in our new routine, albeit a monotonously weird kind of tripping-up-and-stumbling-about normal routine. Our world was starting to feel bland, and worse, it no longer smelled of roses and honeysuckle. We were gradually preparing to take Alice out of hospital, since nothing more could be done for her as an inpatient which couldn't also be done on an outpatient basis. Everything was being organised, and things were set in motion for us to bring her home. The consultant clinical neurologist at Bristol Children's Hospital had written a letter to the social care team noting Alice's symptoms and complex needs. Then they wrote a second letter, which stated that they would not be able to give her their care as Alice would need full-time nursing.

The preparations were under way for an assessment of David and me, together with the boys, for our 'own individual needs'. These would be 'centred on your own state of health and your own physical needs'. So now we were told that we were all in this together. I was made starkly aware of the fact that we were all in need – as if I needed telling.

Over the preceding few weeks, we had had large items of specialised furniture delivered to Valley View Barn. A truck had arrived unannounced one day containing a huge electronic bed, and the guys in the van very kindly lugged it into Alice's room and set it up, plugging it in. It had an attached, handheld control which meant we could move the bed up and down with a few clicks of a button. It also meant that, as Alice was finding it harder and harder to walk and move around, we could position her in the bed and move her into an upright sitting position, while simultaneously raising her legs, so she was less likely to slip down into a slumped horizontal position.

In preparation for moving Alice back to join us in our family home again, we'd also had a hoist delivered. This was to help us get her safely into and out of the bath. We also had a huge, ugly chair so that she could sit comfortably, if a little unattractively, with us in the sitting room. In all our preparations to bring Alice home, I had never been so grateful for and in awe of the NHS. Looking back, the fact that I was getting ready for her return to family life seems rather ludicrous. I just wasn't able to see and comprehend how dramatically her condition was changing for the worse.

Alice had been in the RUH and Bristol Children's Hospital for five months before we knew for certain that she was dying. In fact, we only discovered five days before she died that she was going to go.

I can't exactly remember the moment we were told. I remember where and when we were told that she was ill with pneumonia, and I remember hearing from one of her doctors that they had tried everything, including all the different antibiotics, to treat it. I was there when the physio massaged Alice, trying to get her to expel the water from her lungs. I hadn't understood what he was doing; ludicrously, I hadn't realised how grave the situation was.

I did, of course, know how severe pneumonia could be, but I had never heard the word mentioned in connection with Alice before. My mother had died in Reading at the Royal Berkshire Hospital from pneumonia. I had been joking with the physio, as he was trying to help Alice to cough. I remember telling him that there was no way Alice would 'cough up' or cough on demand. I thought he had been asked to clear her lungs because she had a cold. For a 'normal' child I was sure all the things he was doing would have worked, but they weren't working for Alice, and I had no idea what he was there for and why it was so vital.

The beginning of the end of Alice's life happened one morning. We were at home in Bath, and David was about to leave for a work trip, starting with a round of golf with his bank manager. He was then due to go up to Hull for two days with one of his colleagues. Since we had started David's business, after the first couple of years of marriage, we usually had two or three nights apart during the week. He ran his company from London and was frequently many miles up the M1 in Hull or Beverley; only occasionally did he have a day working from home.

When Alice was in hospital, it was a different story. David still went away on business, but when he was back, I was often not at home, but at the hospital. He would then switch with me, and he sometimes had nights at the hospital, while I went home. We shifted our location according to what was most needed.

This particular morning, we were saying goodbye for an unusual five days. David kept asking me if both Alice and I were going to be OK, as this was the longest time he had been away since she'd been in hospital. In retrospect, it must have been terrifying for him to have to juggle Alice, family and work during those six months.

"Are you sure?" he asked again, even though I'd assured him I was fine. "What about Alice? Do you think she's OK?"

"Of course, darling. I'm sure she's stable. Nothing has changed for such a long time", and I encouraged David to go.

After we'd said our goodbyes, I went straight to the hospital, expecting to start what had become a fairly typical day. One of the neurologists on the medical team would usually pay Alice a visit on his or her morning ward rounds.

It was Dr Saxena's turn; he had been with us the longest and was the on-call doctor that day. We valued and respected him enormously. I didn't think anything was amiss with Alice and I certainly hadn't noticed anything out of the ordinary, but as he left he looked over his shoulder and said casually, "I'll pop by later today to see how things are going."

That fateful day, Wednesday 13th June 2012, was the day when I'd said goodbye to David so unceremoniously, not thinking there was anything too different to what had become routine, but now I had a sudden sense of foreboding.

Dr Saxena's comment had set my alarm bells ringing. In five months, we had never, ever had both a morning and an evening visit. Dr Saxena had been more of a constant presence than any of the other doctors in the neurological team, and for him to do two visits was worrying. Both David and I trusted him and loved his genuine concern for Alice, together with the support he gave us. I suddenly felt very uneasy. I knew Dr Saxena well enough to know that something was properly wrong.

Unbeknownst to me, David was doing well, having reached the ninth hole of the West Course at Wentworth with only one over marked on his card. I rang and he interrupted his game, immediately answering the call.

"David, can you come back? I don't know why, but I think I need you here. Something's wrong." Haltingly, I continued, "Sorry... I can't explain. Please, I think you need to be here, sorry."

I didn't understand why Alice would need a second visit that day, as far as I could see, there was no change in

Alice. After Dr Saxena had left, I realised that I should have asked him to be more specific, to tell me why he wanted to come back. I waited for David as calmly as I could, and he drove as safely as he could.

The drive took two hours, and as soon as he arrived, we talked about the planned second visit from Alice's doctor, and both of us had an intuitive sense that there was something wrong. Meanwhile, Alice was behaving normally and, strangely, our day looked just like any of the other monotonous days we'd spent in the hospital.

Nothing could have prepared us for the shock of Dr Saxena's statement when he arrived later.

"Alice has intractable pneumonia. We've tried every antibiotic; everything possible has been done to help make her better. There's nothing we can do. I'm sorry; she is going to die."

Time stood still.

My mother had died of pneumonia. I couldn't understand how I hadn't seen any of this. How did I not know about these antibiotics that Alice had been having? I thought I knew everything that was happening in her life. I'd met and talked to the physio who had tried to make her cough up, but I hadn't delved deeper to find out what was going on and what he was trying to do.

The following day we were called to be part of a meeting with the doctor in charge of the paediatric intensive care unit (PICU), as well as Dr Saxena and a few of the members of Alice's nursing team. There were six or more of us in that fateful meeting. I called my father, told him what was happening and asked him to come and be with us. I felt I might need his stability and strength to help us make decisions I/we might not be able to make. As it was, he was mostly just a reliable witness to our searing agony and pain, since there were very few choices that we needed to make. I was grateful that I could call him and ask for help; he was able to support the boys, collect them from school and do all the practical things that needed doing.

In the meeting, our questions came thick and fast. The team's statements about what would happen seemed to go even faster.

"She'll need to go into PICU." I don't know who said this.

"Really?" I replied.

"Yes. There's never been a death on the ward where Alice is now," someone said.

"Does she have to go somewhere else?" either David or I replied.

"Yes, she'll need to be on a ventilator," one of the doctors said calmly.

"For how long?" It was probably me who asked this stupid question.

"We've tried everything," someone else said. Another gentle statement that was possibly trying to make us feel better.

"Is there nothing else?" By now, I was trying to grab hold of and clutch those elusive straws.

David was much better in this situation, more systematic and practical with his questions. I was the one who came out with the most awkward or ridiculous questions, inquiries that were a gross testament to my inability to process what was going on.

"If Alice is in PICU, and she is on a ventilator, and we know she can't be made better, who is going to decide when to turn the ventilator off?" A moment of quiet passed, and I asked again, "Who decides when to end Alice's life?"

I couldn't bear the thought of us having to decide when she should take her last breath. It was an abhorrent thought. How could that be expected of anyone, least of all one of her parents?

Then I asked if Alice would be able to stay on the ward, in the room she'd been in for so long. I can't remember who replied. It wasn't the PICU doctor. Most probably it was the matron in charge of the ward. She said she would discuss the situation with the nurses and see if it would be all right with them if Alice died on the ward, and if they would agree to her dying on their watch.

They knew her, had cared for her, had given her everything she needed over the past four months. I wasn't privy to the conversation, but I am forever indebted to the nurses who agreed not to move Alice and let her stay in 'her' room on 'her' ward until the end of her life.

28

The Process

Suddenly, there seemed to be so many decisions for us to make, questions we were posing to ourselves. What should we do about telling her brothers, and how involved should they be? Where would we all be living while this was happening? Should we ask for emotional support for the two of us, as well as the boys? Did we need to be counselled through this nightmare? Did we need extra practical help for Ben and Matthew? How long would it take Alice to die? How long would it go on, and, by the way, does anyone know how long a piece of string is?

The decisions were hurriedly made. The room where Alice had spent the last four months would continue to be her home. David and I would sleep there as well. The PICU nurse, who would be managing her medication and all that went into watching and waiting for a child to die, would be staying in her room for most of the time. When she needed time off, there would be another nurse from PICU to fill in for her.

We were so thankful to the nurses on the ward for their bravery and the way they cared for us and Alice, their young charge. We wouldn't have to move to an unfamiliar place where there was no cheerful bunting or 'Get Well' cards and none of the personal touches that I had spent months gradually accumulating. It was a relief that we wouldn't have to move from this small, friendly space we had made our temporary home.

My father was going to pick up the boys from school and let them know that their sister wasn't well. He can't remember now whether he told them that she was dying and Ben can't remember either, which illustrates how their memories have healed and been tempered. The adage that 'time heals' comes to mind. Having collected the boys, my father took them home to gather a few belongings, clothes, underwear and pyjamas, and then the plan was for him to bring them to the hospital.

I recently asked Ben about what happened that day. He can't remember many details, although soon after it had happened, he told me that someone had come into his classroom to tell him that the headmaster wanted to see him. He was racking his brain wondering why the head wanted to see him, and what on earth he had done wrong. Now he says my father met him and told him about Alice and the need for him and Matthew to come and stay with us in Bristol Children's Hospital.

As is typical of Ben, his reaction was calm and mature for his age. He scooped up his younger brother, and they both went home with my father to collect anything they thought they might need for the hospital for… they had no idea how long. The ward had allocated a room for Ben, Matthew and my devoted father to all stay together. Again, we could not have wished for better care from the hospital and its employees.

When we were all staying in the hospital, the boys had similar beds in their ward room to the one we'd had delivered to our house in Bath in expectation of Alice coming home. These soon became toys and provided a crazy amount of fun for both boys. Matthew would lie flat on his bed, raise one end and then the other, make himself as small as possible and, using the electronic controls, fold himself in half like a sandwich. He'd then push a hand through the sheets and blankets and wave enthusiastically while his body remained invisible inside the doubled-up mattress. Just hearing his muffled giggles from the depths of the bedding and watching the bed shake uncontrollably was a refreshing release from the devastating sadness that was enveloping and engulfing us. Other times, when we were all sitting beside Alice on her mattress designed to prevent bedsores, it would jerk into noisy action and start groaning beneath us. We laughed about the 'dragon' that reputedly slept under the bed, and how we must have disturbed it as it was moaning and complaining about its disrupted sleep. It possibly doesn't sound funny now, but

I tried to keep the boys as entertained as possible, and it helped to alleviate some of the tension.

Alice's ward was brand new, and unusual in that everyone had their own room, or a room that was shared with a maximum of only four children. Ben and Matthew ended up spending five nights sharing a room with their grandfather a few doors down from Alice. There was no 'public' area, and everything was hidden away behind closed doors. The boys were still so young, at eight and ten. Every Sunday, instead of them kicking a football about, or bowling and batting with their father in the cricket net, while Alice and I, together with our Jack Russell and Labrador, played in the village playground, our family was trying to fill time while trapped in Alice's minuscule hospital room.

Our cousin's friends from Bath, Rick and Cathy, were unbelievably generous with their time. We never had to ask them to come to the hospital. They would text us to say they were coming and would often take the boys into Bristol to see local attractions, and inevitably end up having lunch at Ben and Matthew's favourite hamburger bar. Sometimes Rick and Cathy took the boys to the docks, or to see a film; anything to keep them amused. We were so grateful to them and will never forget the kindness and compassion they showed us when we were in a very dark and lonely place.

A nurse, Frances, from PICU, was chosen to be with us to help manage the whole mystifying waiting-to-die procedure. The matron in charge reassured us that she would be excellent at overseeing the process and would be able to cope with the unfamiliar situation of a death being managed on the ward. Primarily, her job was to give Alice the medication that she'd need to make her as comfortable as possible, all while her lungs were shamelessly filling up with liquid.

The boys' hospital room was close to ours. David would remain at the hospital too, and would stay with Alice and me. He had understandably put all his work on hold.

The social care side of the hospital went into full swing, and the boys were asked if they wanted to make memory boxes, which they duly filled with pieces of Alice's hair as well as cards with coloured imprints of her hands and feet. What an extraordinarily ludicrous experience it was to be choosing a lock or two of Alice's soft, wavy, beautiful, beautiful hair, and to have to cut some of it off to put into their memory boxes.

Everything went smoothly. Most of the decisions about what would happen next were made for us and it turned out that there weren't many for us to make at all. Very soon Frances arrived from PICU and Alice was put on a forced ventilator to help her breathe as her lungs were filling up with liquid. Within a day she tried to push the noisy ventilator away and even to take it out, so Frances gently removed it. Alice wasn't being given any more food, so the intranasal gastric tube was taken from her nose and stomach. It was lovely to see her with no plastic tubes emanating from her nose. Sadly, I could now clearly see the bloating in her face, which was a result of the steroids she was taking. With no tubes and nothing foreign, Alice was pure, and, with the pain relief, she was peaceful.

I remember once sitting with her, and, as I was holding her hand, I noticed it had a blue tinge. I looked towards Frances and asked her what we should do about this; it shows how far from reality I was living. Frances gently explained that Alice's body was shutting down, and that this was an entirely normal side effect. Together with her laboured breathing and her lungs filling up, it was apparent to everyone else what was going on; perhaps I was still hoping that it wasn't true, that maybe it was a mistake and Alice might be OK. I was living a life I didn't want to be living.

I mentioned to David, once we knew Alice was going to die and there really was no hope that she could be made better, that I thought it would happen perfectly. From early on, I never felt that Alice was a mistake; more than that, I knew she was purposed and chosen. I knew that a powerful and loving God was sensitively managing everything.

It might sound strange now that I felt God said she was His, yet she was disabled. I have peace with this, knowing that we live in a chronically disabled world. I never questioned what I had been given to cope with, however hard. Even though I have known His love since my early twenties, I still have no explanation for what happened to Alice. I am grateful that I wanted His presence and didn't try to push Him away. I am thankful that He was there all the time; I will be forever grateful that He never once left my side.

Soon after we knew what was happening – that she was going to die – we decided that we should speak to Alice. We needed to explain what we now knew. It sounds crass and not at all amusing, but I would joke with her about the fact that one day, when we were both in Heaven, she would be able to talk to me and correct my pathetic knowledge of her and my assumptions about her likes and dislikes. As it was, I had no idea how to get into her head. I could only guess what she felt or liked or loved, and consequently, I frequently apologised to her for my painful inadequacy. Somehow, I was utterly convinced that she understood most of what was said, and I would talk to her as if she was like any other nearly six-year-old.

Soon after we knew the full facts about what was going on, and what was going to happen, we sat on her bed to talk to her; to try to explain.

David started: "Alice, darling, we have something to tell you. We are so sorry – we and the doctors have tried everything to make you better, but you're not getting better, and worse than that, you are not going to get better. The doctors can't fix you; we just can't heal you… the illness you have is going to take you away from us…"

Alice's eyes were transfixed on David.

He continued, "Alice, sweetheart, we adore you. You are the most beautiful and wonderful daughter. Darling, I hate having to tell you, but your Heavenly Father is calling you home. I cannot look after you properly here, but He is perfect and loves you even more than we do. He made you, and He wants to take care of you. You are going to leave us and go to Him. You'll be there with Mummy's mum, and John Eddison (he had been like a grandfather to David and was the vicar who married us). We will join you as soon as we can. We will hate being apart from you, but your Heavenly Father is amazing, and He will take great care of you."

I stared at her, utterly swept up by her trusting, beautiful little face.

David spoke again, and this is a rough transcript, since I can't recall properly what was said. "You are going to leave us for a time."

While he spoke, Alice's eyes never left him.

"We are so sorry."

Alice turned her attention to me.

I can't recall what I said, if indeed I said anything at all. I'm sure if I did say something, my words were stumbled and trite and thoroughly inadequate.

We carried on talking to her in the same vein, although I hope that what we said was more eloquent than the words I've recorded here. Understandably, I didn't make a note of what was said that dreadful day in her room. It wasn't something I thought I would ever want to remember.

Both David and I can remember Alice looking first at David and then at me, then back to David and then me again. She was concentrating hard on David's words, and seemed to be searching for reassurance and confirmation from me, too. This conversation must have gone on for about ten minutes, maybe more. The way Alice looked at us, her body language, the way she moved her eyes and her head, left us in no doubt that she understood what was being said to her. She understood almost as much as any of us can. She understood in her own way what we were trying to tell her. David talked about a new place for her, somewhere we would one day join her, and we would be together again. A place without sorrow. We told her about the verse in the Bible which describes it:

> And God will wipe away every tear from their eyes; there shall be no more death, nor sorrow, nor crying. There shall be no more pain, for the former things have passed away.
>
> Revelation 21:4

Somewhere around this time, I began to experience a certain degree of peace. I felt I knew that, just as the place for her death was already chosen, so would be the day, the hour, the minute; and, not only that, but it would be the best it could be in such an horrific time. I don't know why I felt this; I just knew we were going to be carried and sustained through it all. This didn't mean that it wasn't unspeakably sad; only that we would be comforted.

On a practical note, Frances had told us that, once various physical signs were evident in Alice, we would probably have twenty to thirty minutes until she took her last breath. We couldn't have asked for anyone better to help us through this. Frances was always reassuring and honest, calm and emotionally unwavering.

Bizarrely, despite the circumstances, or probably because of them, David and I also developed a weird sense of black humour. Nothing was funny, and yet everything was. So, amongst the tears and unbelievable sadness, we quietly laughed at nothing and other ridiculous nothings.

One example of the inappropriate humour we found from nowhere, I hope to be able to convey appropriately: a day or so after we were informed that Alice would die, we were asked if we wanted to donate some of her body parts to help other children who were in need. We were asked to give her heart valves as well as her optic nerves, which are often desperately needed. We painfully deliberated over this request overnight, and took it very seriously. With a great deal of sadness, we decided that we would have to, and now actually wanted to, allow her beautiful body to be cut up for the benefit of another child.

The following day we gave our permission for the harrowing task of Alice being cut open and parts of her being removed for other children's needs – our beautiful little girl, maimed for others. But we had hardly finished speaking when we were told that her body parts couldn't be accepted as there was still no clarity as to what was wrong with her, and it was felt to be too dangerous. This was where our newly acquired, tasteless black humour began! How could we be told that parts of our precious and perfect daughter were desperately needed, and now suddenly she was not good enough?!

Neither David nor I can remember exactly what the things were that we laughed about, but this was undoubtedly one of the times when our humour reared its ugly head. I think we'd got to the point where there was nothing else to do; everything else, just everything, was too agonising.

We were then offered an autopsy. In the same breath, we were told it was improbable that the doctors would find anything out from it, seeing as everything about Alice had been checked already. It was thought to be pointless. Funnily enough, this was something we also rejected.

Our little eight-year-old Matthew would sometimes hurtle into our room first thing in the morning to see if we were all OK. His usual question, "Is she dead yet?", could be more accurately translated as, *How much longer can I bunk off school?* We could never have reprimanded him, and it is a testimony to how close we had become as a family during Alice's time with us. We understood the boys' need to make sense and light of a situation that was as distressing for them as it was for us. It was another moment of wry comedy for us, which David mentioned when he spoke at Alice's funeral. Having a child's perspective on the sad events taking place around us was refreshing, and helped to pull us back to find peace and solace in the land of the living.

29

The Death

When her final moments came, I was sleeping beside Alice in her bed, holding her in my arms. I was woken by Frances carefully telling me that Alice was going. I jumped out of bed and quickly woke David, who was asleep on the pull-out bed by the window in her room. Suddenly we were both sitting together with Alice in our arms. We held her and spoke lovingly to her for her last two breaths. It was quicker, so much quicker than we'd expected. Then she was gone. Just two breaths, not the twenty minutes or so that we had expected.

Only two breaths. Then gone.

I kept an eye on her as I turned to Frances for confirmation. Then I withdrew to the en-suite bathroom, shell-shocked.

I had previously asked Frances if, when the time came, she could bathe Alice, as I thought I wouldn't be able to do it. But now, as I was standing on my own in the tiny bathroom, I realised that I desperately wanted to be the one to wash her. I wanted to get her ready, as I had done nearly every day of the 2,094 days of her life.

I opened the door of the bathroom and told David and Frances that I wanted to 'prepare' her. I asked David if he wanted to join me in washing her and dressing her in the clothes we'd chosen for her to be buried in. He agreed.

As we washed her, her body was still warm. Then we dressed her in her T-shirt with the words *I Love Being Me* on the front, and a pair of matching leggings.

I felt as if I was being swept up in a bad dream. I had a list of things that I had to do, and, as soon as I'd finished doing one, there was something else to do. I was on autopilot as I carried out these sad, mundane, totally surreal and superfluous tasks. All the time I was saying to myself, *Don't catch David's eye, only talk if you absolutely have to, don't engage in the reality of losing her.*

We woke the boys – well, I'm not sure; I think Frances went to wake the boys and my father, and tell them that Alice had just died. But my father has written that it was David who woke him. It's terrible! Both David and I have lost these finer details that I thought would be irrevocably seared in our memories for the rest of our lives.

Before Alice died, David and I had discussed what we thought should happen when she went, and agreed that it would be the best thing for Ben and Matthew if they saw her. We felt it might help them to adjust to the reality of her death. They'd both lived through so much with her and with us, and we thought it would be unnecessarily heartless for us not to trust them with this last goodbye. Matthew now thinks he slept this last night with Alice. I don't want to disabuse him of this belief as it means such a lot to him, and should I really care whether his memory or mine is correct in this matter or not? He can read this book one day and decide which memory he wants to hold on to. There are only a few absolutes in this world, and one of these is that Alice is no longer here.

Ben, Matthew and my father quietly opened the door to our room, said their gentle goodbyes to Alice, and then went back to bed. Having finished dressing Alice, David and I walked through the hospital, wheeling her body carefully on her bed, led by Frances to the mortuary. Alice had died at 4am, which meant no one was awake and we were able to walk through the hospital in peace. We didn't have to conceal the stark reality of our child's death and her empty shell of a body. Had she died during the day we would have had to go through all the corridors and back-room areas, hiding her from the appalling possibility of watching others in the hospital subconsciously rubbernecking.

Once we got to the designated room and left her bed

with her body on it, I began to cry. I cried, as I am crying now, at the memory of that morning and because our beautiful daughter, a very well-loved and treasured little girl called Alice, is gone forever from this world.

A short while later, day broke, and we were back in Alice's bedroom with Frances. There was nothing to say and, even though we'd had five days to adapt to what was happening, both David and I were finding it hard to adjust to the trauma of what we had just witnessed. The early morning sun shone through the window and bounced around my empty heart.

We gathered up Ben and Matthew, and my dear father left to drive himself home. He had now spent five days away from his regular busy routine.

We left Alice's body, left her room untouched, left the hospital and stopped for petrol at a garage in Bath. I can remember the scene vividly. Other customers at the petrol station were going about their daily business as if nothing had happened. I felt like shouting, *Stop! What are you doing?! Our daughter has just died. Stop!* I couldn't understand how life could go on so casually; not that I actually said anything. I knew life would never be the same again for us. Everything about that morning was so final, so painful and so entirely overwhelming.

I arrived home to the onerous task of calling a few close friends to tell them that Alice had gone, that she had died. I think I mostly texted, since I was unable to talk coherently, and there was far too much to talk about and explain. David contacted our local friends as well as some friends in London, Hampshire, Rutland and Bath, some of the places where we had lived with Alice; friends who knew her and had travelled with us along part of the scary road that we'd been on with her. He also called some close friends and relatives abroad. He kept it brief and never asked for a reply to the funeral attendance question. He asked them to spread the word that she'd died and told them that we would send out the date and details about the funeral later.

Somehow, I managed to hold myself above the horror that I was experiencing, and I moved round in a dreamlike state, not daring to look up or down. One conversation I remember very clearly was with a friend from university, Alice. I'd known this Alice since I was about nineteen. She was one of those larger-than-life people who are always full of fun. She'd been a fashion editor at *Elle* magazine, which meant she'd travelled the world to glamorous locations for photo shoots, and I always loved her exotic stories. We'd been in close contact during our Alice's illness, so she was up to date with the situation. When I told her that Alice had died, there was a sharp, dramatic intake of breath from her end of the telephone.

"Oh, no!" she spluttered. "Sorry, darling. On Father's Day. Poor, poor David. I'm so sorry..."

I was in shock. I had no idea that it was Father's Day.

I hadn't been in the real world for a very long time, and it had been months since I had seen anything other than Alice's fitting and drug sheets, as well as studying the doctors' scattered information about her condition.

Strangely, when we were told that she was going to die, I'd had a strong feeling that the date of Alice's death would be a symbolic one for me. However, I hadn't seen anything relevant around the days when it might happen. When we knew she was going to die, I worked out that so far she'd lived for 2,089 days. When she died she had reached 2,094 days, and neither of these numbers, nor those in between, were at all meaningful. I had hoped that the number, whatever it was, would speak to me; say, a random, even 2,090, although this would have had no relevance whatsoever. It just illustrates how I was still trying to find meaning or a reason somewhere, from something or anything at all, that might speak to me.

Also, being a Christian with a leaning towards the Judeo-Christian faith, I had thought that maybe she would die on one of the Jewish feast days, but not one of them were scheduled to happen anywhere around this time. I thought I had searched thoroughly, but obviously, I had missed this one date.

The day she died: Sunday 17th June 2012, Father's Day.

The following day, David and Rick, who had been with us so much during this time, returned to the hospital room and took everything down. There was no way I could have gone anywhere near the place where Alice and I had spent so many minutes, hours, days and months together, never mind the building where I knew her body was still housed. My husband, her adoring father, and Rick took down the bunting, the cards, and gathered up her clothes; everything belonging to our dearest girl. It was this generosity and kindness that we grew to love in Rick and Cathy's friendship. They never asked; they just knew what we needed and did it without question.

At home in Valley View Barn, Charlotte and Naomi, two of Alice's best champions, had become firm friends. Perhaps one of the hardest things I asked them to help me with was sorting out Alice's clothes and toys, now that she had died. I joined them for the first ten minutes of this horrendously painful exercise, and then it dawned on me that I wasn't remotely capable of doing this.

I took a few of the most poignant of Alice's belongings – books we had read together, a toy she often slept with – then mumbled my apologies and entrusted everything else to Charlotte and Naomi to sort, to give away or throw away. They were gracious and loving and just the right people to be able to cope with such a terrible job. As the 'girls' set about the painful job of disposing of all the things that had meant so much to so many of us when Alice had been alive, I withdrew physically and retreated to start my year of weeping and mourning for my only daughter.

30

The Funeral

From the day Alice died, it was as if my brain had been frozen. I was barely able to get myself dressed in the morning, never mind do anything else. The boys had been given compassionate leave from school, so they were at home and, frankly, they kept me sane. David, the competent, calm, organised and gracious man in a crisis, did more or less everything that needed to be done. He found a local funeral director. He chose the church in which to hold the service. He decided on the date and time, and then sent out invitations either by text or email.

Before Alice had died, as her health had become progressively worse, I'd continued to read and reread the words that had spoken to me when I was a brand-new Christian. Silly, perhaps, that I even thought I would find an answer. As I searched, I saw that nothing had told me that she would die. All I could find in the words that I'd had from early on was that my third offspring would be 'surnamed'. This meant nothing at all, or nothing definite at least.

When she was alive, whenever I felt as if things were looking desperate, and voiced my anguish to David, he had always been able to allay my fears. Thus he had kept me from feeling totally lost and hopeless. Had I known she was going to die, I don't know how I would ever have been able to let her go emotionally. David would calm me, I would feel peaceful, and for a few minutes my world, instead of unravelling like a dropped ball of cotton yarn, looked like it was going to remain relatively stable, possibly something I could make into a jumper.

Now she was gone, my husband's calmness and gentle authority had the same effect on my bruised soul. I still continued to read and reread the words that I felt God had given me all those years ago, to see if they offered me an explanation for everything that had happened. Was her death mentioned? Had I missed it? What about the funeral, and what happened next? Again, it seemed senseless that I had placed so much importance on a cluster of verses that hadn't really spoken to me until I found myself pregnant with Alice. I found nothing concrete or anything more than my own assumptions of their personal meaning.

However, within the eighth group of these fifty-six

verses is a non-specific reference, which at this time I interpreted as speaking of the dreaded funeral. It reads:

> "Fear not, for I am with you; I will bring your descendants from the east, and gather you from the west; I will say to the north, 'Give them up!', and to the south, 'Do not keep them back!' Bring My sons from afar, and My daughters from the ends of the earth."
>
> Isaiah 43:5–6

It may sound ridiculous, knowing what we know now, but at this time, these verses told me that somehow our distant friends and scattered family would be coming to her funeral. Even though Alice had been ill for six months, in the end, probably because we hadn't anticipated it, she had died relatively quickly. Everything felt very last-minute, and we had no way of guessing how many would come to the funeral. Only a few had asked about it, and we deliberately hadn't asked for any formal replies. Still, I had a strong sense that we had to get ready for anything. The church had seating for three hundred, so the idea that it could be full for Alice had never seemed likely. Despite this, we ordered three hundred order of service sheets, as well as some postcards with four photos of Alice.

As it turned out, our friends and family came from many different places in the world: Charlie and Sheena (my cousin and his wife) came from Zambia, Shalini (my cousin-in-law) from Kenya, Chantal and Thomas (my cousin and my godson) from France, Mark, my brother and his family from Sweden. David's sister, Sophie, and niece, Annabel, travelled from America; a dear friend of David's, also called David, and his young daughter, Violetta, came from The Hague. Then there was Paddy, who came from work in Spain and joined his wife Susanna in Bath. We also had our friends who had come from all over the UK. The large church was full to overflowing, with standing room only.

On Saturday 30th June 2012, Ben and Matthew calmly stood at the entrance of Holy Trinity Combe Down in Bath, handing out the order of service sheets to our friends and family. Although I hadn't asked her, Sheena's sister, Shalini, who was also a good friend of mine, took photos during the service. She also took some photographic memories at the reception in the marquee afterwards. I was, and remain to this day, so grateful to have these photos, which show all those who were there. Even though I had said hello to everyone at the door of the church, I wasn't mentally present, and it was only when I saw the photos that I realised who had been with us.

It was an incredibly weird situation, standing with my two boys and being thrilled to see close friends and family, some of whom had come from so very far away, in circumstances which couldn't have been worse. I was so happy to see everyone, and yet so utterly devastated that Alice's death was the reason for our reunion. It was strange saying hello to so many I loved, and then goodbye to the one I loved the most.

David chose the food for the reception in the marquee after the church service. Maybe I helped him; possibly I didn't. We had light bites and a few non-alcoholic drinks. With a little bit of involvement from me, David chose the hymns, the layout of the service sheet, and who was going to talk.

David also decided on the vicar to take the service. He had known the Reverend Rico Tice since he was fourteen and they were good friends. During the five months leading up to Alice's death, Rico had been very close to David, ringing him regularly to check how things were going. Having him involved in the service was a comfort to both of us. He'd even altered his jam-packed work plans to fly back to the UK to take the service. The readings were all chosen by Rico; the most input I could manage was, "Yes, sounds good." Although, given the way I was feeling, I have no idea what was coming out of my fraught and wounded mind via my mouth.

David and Chris, Naomi's father (the headmaster of the boys' school), who had become a good friend of ours, organised for the marquee to be placed in front of the school building on one of the playing fields. The school was within easy walking distance from the church, and where we would have the drinks and light bites afterwards. The marquee was placed right on top of the rugby pitch which both Ben and Matthew had played on.

The one thing I know that I did do was choose some photos of Alice which I had taken over the nearly six years of her life. These were then presented during the funeral service via a slideshow set to music. We had five of these photos printed onto large canvases, which were balanced on easels and placed around the marquee. They were reminders of some of the happy times she had given us. Her smile and the love she radiated were captured in them; a little comfort on that harrowing day.

David and I kept calling Alice's funeral 'her wedding', or sometimes just 'the wedding'. We might say to a friend on the phone, something like, "I'll see you at twelve for the wedding." We were confused, irreverent; I'm not sure what. The only logical reason for this could be that we were preparing for the day of the funeral in the same way as we'd planned for our wedding. Choosing a church, choosing hymns, selecting a vicar, printing the service sheets, deciding on food and drinks – it was surreal. She would never be married here. Terrible.

For the opening reading, Rico had chosen a psalm about how loss and tears were the writer's (probably King David's) friends. We had asked Frances, who had nursed Alice to her very last breath, to read this and she'd kindly agreed.

Just as everyone was settling down in the church, David turned to me. "Have you seen Frances?" he said.

I turned around, desperately searching for Frances's face amongst the others. "No, I haven't," I replied.

I scanned everyone around me again, trying not to catch anyone's eye, hopelessly looking for Frances. There was no sign of her.

"I'll do it, David; I'll read the psalm," I whispered.

Suddenly I found myself standing in front of everyone, my swollen, red eyes and my naked grief there for all to see. In the seconds before I stood up, I thought I should just quickly read through Psalm 42 as it wasn't one I was familiar with. I looked at the service sheet, and was horrified to see that there had been an error in the printing. The second page contained the start of the first reading, which was the psalm, but when I turned the page over to finish the last few verses, it went straight to the second reading and omitted the end of the psalm. I was flabbergasted!

We had checked and then double-checked the proofs. We'd had the expense of the marquee, the large photographs, and food and drinks to shell out for, and now I saw that the costly order of service was wrong. I was confused and then devastated. I didn't have enough time to show David, and have a look at his copy. I stood up to read, totally preoccupied with my confusion. I wasn't, on any level, thinking of Alice.

As I faced the congregation, I tried desperately to politely and clearly explain to everyone that there was a problem with the service sheet and that they would have to turn over two pages to find the end of the psalm. David looked at me, caught my attention and signalled for me to be quiet and to carry on and read.

I was still fuming about the service sheet, but I dutifully obeyed him and began reading. The psalm suddenly meant very little to me as I was totally preoccupied with the confusing service sheet. I couldn't understand how this could possibly have happened. I was reading meaningful, touching words like 'Why is my soul so downcast within me?', but the words I was reading were eclipsed by the thunderous voice in my head saying, *I'll tell you exactly why it's downcast. The order of service sheet is* wrong! *After all that trouble and all that care, it's all messed up!*

I carried on with the reading, though the words weren't speaking to me any more – 'My tears have been my food day and night…' – and I still couldn't focus because my scattered brain was stuck in a baffled riot. *How could this have happened? This has spoilt everything that we have planned so meticulously.*

After I finished reading, when I sat down next to David, I looked at his service sheet, and it was just as it should have been. Then I checked the ones the boys had, and they were fine. No one else's but mine was wrong. I will never understand this, and I lost the service sheet anyway. I lost it when I had to leave it on the seat. I lost it when I woke Matthew, then held his hand to go and follow the coffin. I never saw it again – a metaphor, perhaps, for Alice's life with us; always a mystery, and then she was gone.

Looking back now, I can, of course, ask, *Did it really matter?* At the time, in those few minutes when I was reading the psalm, it really mattered. But this strange mix-up did serve a purpose: while trying to read in front of everyone, my mind had been diverted from the gruelling job at hand. My thoughts had gone off on a tangent to worry needlessly about a minor mistake, it turned out it was only my copy that was wrong!

After the readings, we had asked David's father, Anthony, as a close and loving grandfather to Alice, to begin by saying the prayers, which he did in his uniquely beautiful way. Annabel, David's niece, then got up to speak. Although she'd already had most of her life in the States and we hadn't had much time with her, she felt very close to her cousin.

Years before, Annabel had been the first and probably the only person to tell me she thought I was pregnant with a girl; the fact that she has an older brother as well as four male first cousins might have played a powerful part in her helpful prediction. Annabel was like an older sister to Alice and, during occasional visits, they had spent most of their time playing and laughing as if they'd never been apart. As she spoke, she was calm and loving, with a confidence way beyond her years. It always surprises me how children take death in their stride. She was six months shy of twelve years old, and I was so proud of all that she said about our daughter.

Annabel said that she and Alice always talked about the next time they would 'visit' – a good Americanism. Then she said, "I'll have to wait for Heaven now. I loved that we were like sisters."

The very last thing Annabel gave us was an acrostic poem, *ALICE W*:

A: Adored by everyone.
L: Loved by Jesus.
I: In Heaven with Jesus.
C: Cherished by us.
E: Enriched our lives.
W: Will miss her very much.

There was applause for her bravery and her moving words about her cousin.

Then it was Naomi's turn to talk. As I've mentioned before, she was the daughter of the boys' headmaster, and I'd first met her when she babysat our three children one night a few years previously. She had become a dear friend to our whole family, and had played a fundamental and important role in the intense journey that we had been on with Alice.

Naomi had come with us to Cornwall the summer before Alice's lengthy stay in hospital, and had always been there to help and listen. When she got up to speak, the love I felt for her was as strong as if she had also been my daughter.

This is a short transcript of what she said:

"One thing, among many, that inspires me, and that I loved and admired about Alice, was that she was just so good about everything. She was so tolerant. She didn't complain. She wasn't demanding.

"But Alice wasn't just good and content – she was joyful; she just revelled in life. She was such a beautiful, happy little girl. Alice had a lot to contend with, but always had a smile on her face, and she definitely spread that smile to those who spent time with her.

"I loved being with Alice in Cornwall. It was so wonderful to see her enjoying herself so much. Cornwall was a place where she was really happy. Alice really enjoyed walking on the beach; I think she liked the feel of the sand between her toes, and the sea breeze in her face. She loved to be outside, and when it was windy, she would put her face into the wind, close her eyes, open her mouth and squeal in delight. Alice didn't take little things for granted. I think what she really liked about Cornwall was the vast expanse of sand where she could wander as she pleased. I would often take her hand in mine to offer some support as she walked, but Alice liked her independence and would always pull away as if to say, *Thank you... but I'll be fine*. And her determination saw her through most of the time. I think she liked that feeling of freedom on the beach.

"Alice also loved to swim... no matter how cold it was! I would tentatively dip a toe in the pool and shiver just at the thought! She was a bit tougher than me. She didn't bat an eyelid at the cold! But every time I took the plunge, it was always worth it – Alice just loved it so much!"

I have recently listened to the tape we have of the funeral service, and it's striking how much is lost when you only have the words. What I have recorded here is from a paper copy of her speech that Naomi sent me, but hearing it again has been deeply poignant. What is missing from the printed version is the crashing silences.

Naomi stopped several times during her eulogy when she became overcome with emotion. Her voice broke frequently, and several times she had lengthy moments when she was unable to speak. At the time there were several points when I thought she wouldn't be able to continue at all. Once, when I heard her voice giving up, possibly for the fourth or fifth time, and saw her staring tearfully at her notes, unable to speak the words she had so tenderly written, I turned and whispered to David, "I just can't bear her pain; I have to go and stand with her." I stood up and went and put my arm around her, and then I started the line she was struggling to read. Naomi smiled weakly at me as I read the words she could no longer manage. We both knew that we had shared so many jobs in Alice's life, and now we were doing the same in her death.

I continued the sentence for Naomi: "We'd spin around together..."

Naomi carried on: "She'd playfully pat the water with her hands, splashing and splashing and squealing. I'm sure, like the beach, she loved to be free in the water. I've thought about Alice such a lot recently. I miss hearing her happy noises, I miss watching her cuddling Moo Cow and sucking her thumb, I miss reading *A Squash and a Squeeze* to her. I miss giving her cuddles and hearing her giggle. It's such a deep sadness that she's no longer with us, but what comforts me is such an unbelievable thought – that she's now with her Heavenly Father, and she's totally free. She's enjoying to the full that glimpse of freedom that she felt on the beach and in the water.

"I think being with Alice changed me. I really feel inspired by her love of life, and I feel privileged to have spent so many precious moments with her."

Together, we then turned around and went to sit down.

Next, it was my father's turn to speak. It's hard to know what to edit out here. He had been waiting at our front door in Rutland, to usher in the midwife the night Alice was born. Then he stayed in the hospital with us when we were waiting for her to die. I can't imagine how hard this must have been, given that his wife had died in hospital of pneumonia and now he was facing watching his daughter burying his granddaughter, who'd also died in hospital of pneumonia. I'm not sure I have the words to describe how grateful I am for his ability not to wallow in his own, very personal tragedy. How grateful I am to him for his strength to share in our intimate grief without overshadowing it with his own story. This is an abridged version of his moving talk.

"Alice was an easy baby, content to lie still and sense the world revolving around her. But doctors investigating her squint found that it was not her eyes but her brain that wasn't working normally. Gradually, we all began to realise that she was very different from most other children – and always would be. About a year ago she started having serious epileptic fits and, after a bad bout over Christmas, she was admitted to hospital. Over the following months of constant seizures, of tests and of powerful medications, she never once complained, rarely cried, and she won the hearts of her carers and visitors. She responded, as she had always done, to touch and sound. Soft caresses, the human voice and music seemed to reach into her innermost being and, when she was free of fits, she was able to communicate her own feelings and reveal her special personality through physical contact, by her giggles and babbles, and by giving us the most gorgeous, warm smiles.

"Short though it was, Alice's life was packed full of joy as well as pain and sorrow. It was full of struggles and hard-won achievements. She attracted from other people the most intense feelings of love, of tenderness and of commitment. She brought out in those around her the finest of human qualities. Who can put a value on such a precious life?"

After my father spoke, the congregation were asked to stand. We then sang the song that we had sung the first few lines of when putting Alice to bed every night; 'My Jesus, My Saviour'.

Now it was David who stood up. A couple of days after Alice had died, David had not been able to sleep. Insomnia was something he'd never experienced before. He got out of bed one evening and then spent the next four or five hours planning the funeral and writing his address.

David's eulogy for his daughter was undoubtedly the most significant and tremendous thing at the funeral. He had been warned by wise and loving friends that he would not be able to do this talk, but he did it because he knew God had written it for him and had asked him to do it. It could not have been better, more sensitive or more honouring of Alice.

David started by thanking all those who had spoken at the funeral; then his parents for their unwavering support. He thanked Rick and Cathy for their constant presence in our lives during those dreadful months in hospital, and then at the end when Alice was dying. His voice was calm and gentle, kind and washed with the warmth of love that was Alice. He thanked our friends and relations for coming, especially given the many miles some of them had travelled. What I'm describing here is still, curiously, sounding like a wedding.

David then addressed Ben and Matthew, his voice breaking as he spoke about how proud both he and I were of them. He told them that they were fantastic sons and had been the best brothers to Alice. He thanked them for being so kind, and went on to describe how patient they'd been when they were dragged off to the hospital over and over again throughout the previous six months. He talked about Alice's love for her brothers, and the joy we had felt on seeing the three of them mucking about together and enjoying each other's company.

He explained that they had both kept us sane in those last few days. He mentioned how Ben would pop into Alice's room to give David an update on the Euro 2012 World Cup news, and there was laughter from all around us. Then he mentioned how Matthew would cheer us up by telling us how he would persuade the nurses to dive into their tuck supply, and how he would appear with yet another ice cream or a can of Coke. More laughter.

Within this most moving talk about our young daughter, David then asked our boys to collect a massive bunch of flowers that he had bought that morning, cross the length of the church and give the flowers to Kay. She had been Alice's godmother and our ever-present comforter and help. Unfortunately, she herself had been ill for most of the time that Alice was in hospital, and she had been having a genuinely tough time. We wanted to say thank you and sorry, and to tell her how much we loved her. David said, "No one, apart from Joanna, my wonderful wife, has loved and looked after Alice more than Kay."

The last thing David planned was to ask all Alice's carers to stand up so that we could applaud them and thank them for all they did for Alice and for us. The following impressive list of people got to their feet: a few of those who were able to come from the team at Bristol Children's Hospital; Frances, who managed Alice's death; some of the teachers at Three Ways School; some of the teachers and professionals at BOP; Alice's carers at home; and all her tutors. David read out the names of all the wonderful women who had served Alice, sometimes to a self-sacrificing degree, starting with the one we'd known longest, right through to our most recent friends: Kay, Janet, Amanda, Liz, Jane, Sarah, Caroline, Charlotte, Naomi, Jenny, Katie, Juliet, Rosie and Anna. Many came, and those who were there stood up so we were able to publicly applaud and say an unequalled thank-you to them.

After these tearful and heartfelt thanks, we played a slideshow that I had made of twenty-six photos of Alice, from when she was born to just before she went into hospital. This was set to a song, which the new vicar of the church had suggested, with words and a tune that had recently become so meaningful to us:

I can only imagine
What it would be like
When I walk by Your side.

I can only imagine
What my eyes would see
When Your face is before me.
I can only imagine.
I can only imagine.

Surrounded by Your glory
What will my heart feel?
Will I dance for You, Jesus,
Or, in awe of You, be still?
Will I stand in Your presence?
To my knees will I fall?
Will I sing hallelujah?
Will I be able to speak at all?

I can only imagine.
I can only imagine.

'I Can Only Imagine', Bart Millard and MercyMe

Then David spoke about who Alice was.

While writing this account of Alice's funeral, I was uncertain about listening to the tape of what David said, as it's so painful to relive the extraordinary emotion that we felt at the time. But I did listen to it, and here is a very abridged excerpt:

"Alice wasn't defined by her disabilities. She had a captivating way of communicating with her eyes and her smile. She had an innate, unquestioning trust in other people. She never demanded attention but was delighted to receive it. It's hard to make sense of all of this. Two weeks ago she died, and four weeks ago we were getting ready to bring her home. It's hard to contemplate life without Alice. She was at the heart of our family, and she was the heart of our marriage."

Our lovely friend Rico then spoke in a way that only he can; he spoke honestly and with his whole heart, and we were very grateful for his friendship and love through this unbearable time.

As soon as it was all finished, just as the music started to signal the end of the service, I realised Matthew had fallen asleep on my lap. I woke him gently, and we filed out of the church, following Alice's body, encased in a simple wicker coffin decorated with a single baby-pink peony.

I felt completely empty and numb after the weird and devastatingly moving experience we had all just been through.

There is nothing more to say.

31

The Burial

The interment was to be the following day in the churchyard at St John's Church, Hinton Charterhouse. We had never been to this particular church, but it was next to the cricket ground and the playground that we'd visited nearly every weekend since we'd moved to Bath.

A peculiar thing had happened to me after the funeral. I had almost completely forgotten that we still needed to have the burial. I knew during the funeral that we weren't going to bury Alice the same day, but I hadn't mentally adjusted to the massive implications of the tragic and final burial of her body in the ground.

After the funeral, when it came to discussing the practicalities and organisation of the burial, even though it was probably easier than planning the funeral, I felt overwhelmed with exhaustion and unable to face the task of going through yet more pain. My husband, who remained lovingly reliable and calm during this awful time, once again picked up the heavy mantle willingly.

Unlike the day of the funeral, which was sunny and bright, the day of the burial was drizzly and cold. Most sombre for the beginning of July. We had only invited a select few friends and family members. We felt that most of the people who mattered had come to the funeral and to enforce yet more sadness upon them so soon was unnecessary. So a motley crew of just over fifteen were there: David and me, our boys, David's parents, my father and one of my brothers, John. Naomi was also there. Charlie, Sheena and Shalini came, as did their friends, Rick and Cathy from Malawi, who had been so phenomenally kind to us when Alice had been in hospital. A local friend who pulled a few strings and found us a plot in the cemetery was there too, as well as the vicar and obviously the pallbearers.

I just remember feeling an overwhelming sense of unreality. While I was staring at the coffin, I wanted to scream, *It's impossible. She's not gone, she's not in there*, and other inappropriate things like, *Stop!* and *No, no, nooooo!* I wanted to sob and shout. I wanted to fling myself on top of my little girl. In my head I was saying, *Please don't make this happen, please make this not true, please don't put her in the ground... please... just don't let her go...*

I felt overcome with a desire to shout and scream and sob... and yet, of course, my British reserve kicked in, and I did a typical English nothing.

I looked at my sons and saw the grief in their innocent faces and realised that this story was no longer just about me, David and our needs. It was always going to be about a family coming to terms with the death of the one who had been at their very centre. Reluctantly, we walked away from the grave, though none of us wanted to leave her.

A few months later, on Alice's birthday, when we again had occasion to remember her by the side of her grave, I remember Matthew lying on the wet ground on top of Alice's grave, reluctant to leave. Another reminder of the monumental occurrence that had happened in his and his brother's young lives.

On two occasions over the year following Alice's death, Matthew talked at both his schools about his sister. The first time was when we were still in Bath and he and his year group were asked to enter a competition to speak to the whole school at morning assembly about something that really mattered to them. One of his contemporaries talked about bitcoin, another about global warming, and Matthew decided he wanted to talk about his sister and her death.

After they had spoken to their year groups, some were picked to speak to the whole school, and Matthew was one of those chosen.

The next time he spoke in public was after we had moved to Berkshire, less than a year later, at his new school. He spoke eloquently and very genuinely about his sister.

None of us had suggested this to him; it was something he needed to do. There were things he still needed to say. I remember watching him, at the age of eight and then nine, alone on the stage. On both occasions he told the other children the same thing:

"Alice never complained. We complained, but she didn't. And Alice never gave up, especially when it was training time, or when the tutors came round. Many of you will know the game Dizzy Dinosaurs, when you spin around, and the last one standing wins… the occupational therapist told us that we should spin Alice round on a large board as it was good for her senses and also for her brain to focus again after being dizzy. I didn't like doing this, and neither did Alice, but she never gave up."

To witness Matthew speak of his sister and her death, and see his hurt and pain, together with his evident admiration of her, was yet another milestone on our journey.

Do I regret all that happened?

I didn't have a choice.

Do I wish it had never happened?

Every day.

One thing I learned when observing the boys' reactions was the differences they showed in the way they dealt with their grief. Both boys were still at an age where they reacted without any social inhibitions. Neither could yet put on a brave face, or disguise the way Alice's death had affected them.

Matthew has never been afraid to wear his heart on his sleeve, whereas Ben has always been more private but feels just as deeply. I clearly saw that neither boy's reaction was better or worse than the other's. They were just different. I loved that I could, and still can, talk to Ben about Alice without fear of his world falling apart. He is dependable and has always been wise for his years. I came to understand that the loss of their dearly loved sister was just as profound for both of them. They each dealt with her illness and subsequent death in their own way. Perhaps it took something as extreme as Alice's death to illustrate to me just how different my boys are and, more importantly for me, to learn how much I treasure, value and respect their individuality.

At some point after Alice died, I went into Matthew's room and, on his bed, I noticed his handheld whiteboard. He had erased all the notes that usually adorned his board, like his homework and scores in his school sports matches, and had written, 'Alice is the best sister in the world.' And, in the same pen, Ben had added, 'I agree.'

I took a picture of this but I'm not sure when I saw it; I just know that it was one of the most beautiful and tragic things I had ever seen. Possibly it was done when the boys were packing up their clothes to come to hospital. I asked both Ben and Matthew at the time, but neither of them could remember the details.

Alice as an individual, if you take away all that she needed from others to have a voice and to communicate, was a girl who radiated life and laughter, fun and hope. In fact, all the things, and more, that we frantically seek for our own lives. Those who spent time with her were filled with all the goodness and excitement of life that she emanated. Spending time with someone who remains innocent, kind, grateful and loving changes you. The hours and hours I spent in her company were never wasted time – even when things were frustrating and painful. On an emotional level, being with Alice felt, most of the time, like being on holiday. That deep breath of fresh air, those lungfuls of life that you experience when you get to your place of relaxation, were nearly always felt in her presence. To know someone who never wanted more, or anything other than what was going on around her – and, more than that, something that you had chosen for her – was a beautiful and unique experience.

Today, I know where her body is. I know where she's buried. You leave the church cemetery, get into your car and then drive along a single track, then turn right and drive through a hamlet with a village shop and a small post office. Then travel along another road and up a steep hill, passing a magical castle on your right. Then you drive through a stunning city, which has warm, healing baths, naturally filled by thermal groundwater. After this, you go along another long, unremarkable road, up a steep hill, straight across about five roundabouts and onto the motorway at Exit 17, and then off again at Exit 12. Soon you drive past the beautiful, isolated and hidden country church where David and I were married twenty years ago. Without making a diversion, you drive on through a burgeoning village built around a bustling road junction, with a phenomenal butcher by the side of a railway bridge. Trains go over this and can take you to London. You then have to pay 60p for the toll bridge. When I first went over the bridge, the toll was only 2p. I learnt to kayak on the Thames, under this bridge and near a weir.

You are welcome to visit Alice's grave any time if you can figure out the directions in reverse from here, and I can visit her grave too. You might not want to go as some of the ground where the bodies are buried seems to be subsiding, and their silent tombs and broken gravestones are tipping and crowding in, one over another.

David and our boys sometimes like to go to Alice's grave, and they take flowers. I go with them, but don't like to. For me, the grave is just a reminder that the ground houses the remains of her body, and it is a gruesome reminder that Alice's shell is deteriorating. For that reason, I hate going there; I hate the fact that my overactive imagination runs wild. I have to tame and silence the gruesome images that leap up and try to badger me unawares. David and the boys see the grave for what it is: a place of peace and tranquillity, and a place to remember and find joy in the memories of the happy girl who was their daughter and their sister.

Alice's place in my life couldn't be more apparent to me. Right at the beginning of my pregnancy, during my anguish, God said that this child belonged to Him; He claimed her as 'His child'. After that, she was born with the red 'kiss' – her 'salmon patch' – on her wedding ring finger. Then there were the promises about my three 'offspring' in the Bible that God had shown me when I was in my early twenties, and which I rediscovered when I was thirty-six. There were also the verses about Him bringing those from afar and the ends of the earth, which I randomly took to speak of the packed church for her funeral. Probably one of the best pieces of the puzzle of Alice's life was confirmed by the fact that I will always know that she died on Father's Day. It helps me to think that she's gone home to be with her Father; it helps me to remember that she always belonged to Him.

I'm glad I wasn't aware that Father's Day was coming up when she was dying, or I would have been totally transfixed by that date. When I think about this now, although it moves me, it still doesn't mean quite enough. It doesn't alter the fact that she has, quite simply, just gone.

I still lost her.

In this world, we are confined by the framework of the clock as we know it. We're stuck in this thing called time, and so we can't understand what it means to live outside of this restriction.

It might sound peculiar, but I have solace.

I know that, now and for eternity, Alice is with God.

It is also somewhere that, one day, we will be with her again.

32

After Death

About a year after Alice died, we made a big move to Berkshire, away from the excruciating memories of Alice and all that she represented in me and us. I now needed a complete change and a hope that life would be better for all of us. David would be much closer to work and our family, and we wouldn't have to have nights apart. We enrolled the boys at Elstree Prep School. It was definitely a very good move for all of us, and as I later found out, many families who lose a child, choose to move area.

When Alice died, many people asked if I felt angry. Some asked if I thought that my faith was being tested; if David was also struggling with his belief in a compassionate God. Other questions included, "What about counselling? And for the boys?" Of course, these are reasonable questions with realistic assumptions for our sudden needs, but it was never the case that I questioned God's presence or that we felt we needed outside counsellors.

I did consider counselling, but am very fortunate to have a husband and children who are frank in spilling out their emotions and not shy with their uncomfortable questions. Many of these inquiries I am not ashamed to leave sitting in an open drawer, resting beside the unattainable answers.

The one thing I found very hard, was explaining to my 'new' friends, how many children I had. A common question that is batted around at the school gates, as mums get to know each other and place one another in relevant boxes. The first time I was asked how many children I had, I was taken by surprise, and as the tears hurried to the surface of my eyes I knew I needed to find a way to explain that I had two boys, well, but I had three children, except no! I didn't. Over time this became easier, as I learnt to gauge the context of the question as well as the situation I was standing in. Sometimes I could take my time, and I could talk honestly and openly about our daughter's death, and sometimes all I needed to say was "I have two sons." This was not an easy lesson to learn.

At the moment I am reading a book by a boy called Jonathan, who is near the age Alice would be if she were still alive today. He was unable to communicate for years and years, and yet his parents held on to the opinion that he was really in there, just trapped by his severely dysfunctional body. It was their commitment and determination that allowed them to teach him to communicate, which in turn enabled him to type laboriously just by using his eyes.

His book is a beautiful revelation of the inner workings of someone who knows what is essential in life. Just through reading his words, and hearing in them the distant voice of my daughter, I am more heartbroken than I can possibly say.

As I read this book, I am sitting waiting in a cold garage for my car to be serviced, and I am overcome with sorrow that Alice was never able to talk to me. When Jonathan writes about the choice he made to come back from his vision of Heaven to live in his broken body for his family, I am speechless with gratitude to him and his mother and family, who are all fighting the fiercest of fights. They are such awesome examples of love, sacrifice and the decision to dedicate themselves to a reality that is a huge burden to bear. Having said that disability is a burden, which of course it is, it is a burden crowned with greatness, courage and love. One that I feel I have shared, and one that I feel honoured to have been chosen to live for a time. Thank you, dear Bryan family, and especially to Jonathan, for making your incredible self known. I will be forever grateful.

Time and again, Jonathan cheated death, and his following words resonate with my gratitude to him:

I had been given extra time so that I could use my voice to make a difference for the voiceless.

Eye Can Write, Jonathan Bryan

As far as my faith goes, I had already lived enough, and known God for long enough, that I had no need to question His goodness and love, not even for a second. David, likewise, knows his God. As far as counselling goes, we talk. John Eddison once memorably said, "David talks until he finds something to say." This has always made his close family laugh, and without this trait, he, I and our boys would probably be buried deep in 'therapy debt.' David keeps me honest and open when perhaps I would stay in denial and remain silent.

We live in a grieving and unjust world. A visitor from another planet would only need to switch on the TV to immediately witness the brutality and injustice that dominate. It is blatantly apparent that so much in this world is horrendous. Is it fair that I blame God for this? And should I blame God for Alice's difficulties? Is this not the injustice that is the result of our decision to exercise free will and do the things that we know we shouldn't do?

There was nothing in particular that stood out for me when we faced the shock of Alice's unexpected death. It was a combination of deep sadness, sorrow, grief, loss and the insurmountable pain which patterned my darkest days. Even now, the emptiness is immense, though the sense of unreality is somehow diminishing with time.

I do have an unshakeable belief that I will see Alice again. It is all a mystery, one that was hidden in her in so many ways, for not nearly enough days. I don't feel mine is to question why. Mine is to continue to stand up, love and serve my Lord. To continue to fight to be loving and gracious to others, even when I hurt inside.

I have been many incarnations: the newly-wed wife with strong expectations, full of youth and vibrancy; the proud, exhausted mother who started a traditional busy family with two delightful boys; a bemused and scared mum of a disabled child; and finally, a forever-grieving individual who has an aching loss.

After Alice died, we were sent two copies of this poem, by local friends in Bath, and I can't resist putting it in this book. It always moves me to tears and communicates the truth in a way that I feel unable to.

> I will lend you, for a little time,
> A child of mine, He said.
> For you to love the while he lives,
> And mourn for when he's dead.
> It may be six or seven years,
> Or twenty-two or three.
> But will you, till I call him back,
> Take care of him for Me?
> He'll bring his charms to gladden you,
> And should his stay be brief.
> You'll have his lovely memories,
> As solace for your grief.

I cannot promise he will stay,
Since all from earth return.
But there are lessons taught down there,
I want this child to learn.
I've looked the wide world over,
In search for teachers true.
And from the throngs that crowd life's lanes,
I have selected you.
Now will you give him all your love,
Nor think the labour vain.
Nor hate Me when I come
To take him home again?
I fancied that I heard them say,
"Dear Lord, Thy will be done!"
For all the joys Thy child shall bring,
The risk of grief we'll run.
We'll shelter him with tenderness,
We'll love him while we may,
And for the happiness we've known,
Forever grateful stay.
But should the angels call for him,
Much sooner than we've planned.
We'll brave the bitter grief that comes,
And try to understand.

A Child of Mine, Edgar Guest

Epilogue

Autumn

2020

My MS didn't really resurface until Alice died. I didn't tell either of my sons that I had this illness until it became evident about eighteen months after we had left Bath. Unfortunately, I made a few errors after she died, ignoring all the things I knew I should do in terms of managing my health. I think part of me gave up trying. Perhaps this was a result of the exhaustion, grief and my deep sorrow. I was not thinking.

I had a stem cell transplant three years ago to try to halt the progression of the disease, which was raging its full force upon me. Now I walk with a stick, I am sometimes in a wheelchair, and have little or no balance. My husband has been amazing as it has been a very tough road for him.

Both our teenage boys are coping seamlessly and remain a constant source of joy and strength to me.

Life potters on, there is still so much to be thankful for.

There is one passage, the penultimate one in the words given to me, now twenty-nine years ago, that speaks of God doing 'a new thing'. There are fourteen verses in this passage that clearly speak of Him displaying His power. I would love for this to be my miraculous healing.

Alternatively, I might have to continue to rest on the two Bible verses that have been my indomitable 'go-to's through a mountain of difficulties.

The first, taken from a verse in the Book of Job (the oldest book in the Bible), is spoken when Job has lost everything. He has had a terrible time of illness, pain and suffering. He has also lost all of his children, together with his material wealth. His friends are emotionally absent, and his wife offers no support; telling him to give up. Job says about his faith in God:

> Though He slay me, yet I hope in Him.
>
> Job 13:15

The second is another verse I have held on to when in need of support. It is taken from the Book of Daniel, which was recorded in about 618 BC when he was a young man. Daniel and his three friends are about to be thrown into a fiery furnace for refusing to worship Nebuchadnezzar's objects of idolatry. He says:

> Our God whom we serve, is able to deliver us from the burning fiery furnace... but if not, let it be known to you, O king, that we do not serve your gods, nor will we worship the gold image which you have set up.
>
> Daniel 3:17

My latest comforting passage, which I only discovered more recently but have since learnt, is from Psalm 27, Verse 13: I remain confident of this: I will see the goodness of the Lord in the land of the living.

These three passages and many more in the New Testament have kept me safe and free to be who I was made to be, regardless of what my body sometimes says! Many years ago, I chose to give God the authority over my life, and I am determined to continue to do so, no matter what.

> For now we see only a reflection as in a mirror; then we shall see face to face. Now I know in part; then I shall know fully, even as I am fully known.
>
> 1 Corinthians 13:12

Bless you for reading this story of my daughter's precious life, and, sincerely, thank you for your time.

Acknowledgements

I could not have hoped to have done any of what I did for Alice, without the unwavering support of my husband. I am deeply grateful for his love and his unwarranted confidence in me, and for being the most perfect and loving father to Alice. Thank you too, to our sons. They always took our breath away with their unconditional love for their sister as well as for us.

Thank you to all those who found themselves on the same road we travelled for a time, who held our hands and steadied our feet. Thank you to those who laughed with us, as well as those who wept with us. Thank you to all those who wrote notes for this book. Thank you to those who enabled our daughter and sister to do all she did, with all the joy that she then gave us.

Thank you for all the help with writing this book; most notably thank you to Joe at Troubador Publishing whose patience kept me sane when everything was getting on top of me. Thank you to Alison for running a fantastic creative writing course in Bath, and then later for being my long-suffering editor. Thank you to Antoinette for getting me going and encouraging me to write it all down. Thank you to my friends, Kay, Alice, Richard, Julie, Simon, Rico, David, Grace, Busky, George, Rupert and Abi particularly, who have read, glanced at, skimmed or studied one or more versions of the manuscript and given me wise and much-needed advice. Thank you to Chris and Adelle without whom this manuscript might never have seen the light of day. Thank you to Charlie for loving Alice, supporting us and doing the front cover so magnificently. Thank you all, for your support and encouragement. I am deeply humbled.

Thank You mostly to my Lord and my Saviour, Jesus.

Notes from Those Who Knew Our Daughter

Kay W.

Kay is a dear friend whom I met in 2001, three months after Ben was born. She has been an unsurpassable and gracious mother figure to me and a grandmother for our children, as well as Alice's godmother.

A Letter to Alice

I am thankful that you graced my life, and that I got to see your smile and walk hand in hand with you on the sand in Cornwall. I am thankful to God, who allowed me to see you through His eyes and know that you were more than a little girl with special needs. You shared your love and happiness with so many; a true gift. I was blessed to be your godmother and will miss and love you forever.

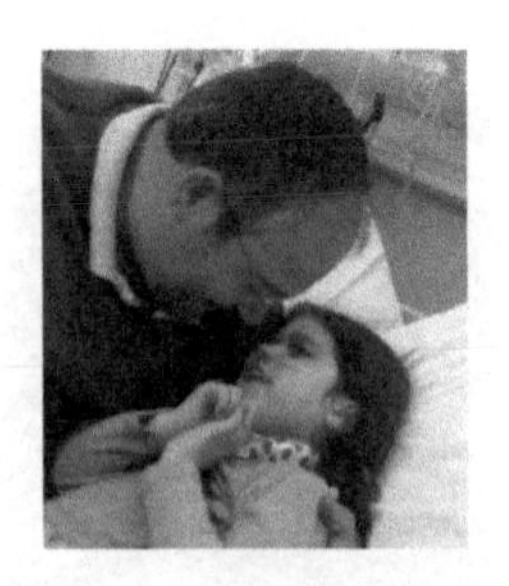

Rick J.

Rick and his wife, Cathy, were our family's constant comfort in Alice's last six months in 2012.

Dear Joanna and David,

Here is my small contribution to Alice's memory book. It's less of an experience and more of something about her that will stay with me always. I'm also attaching a photo of her with David just one week before she died.

Alice brought out the very best in people. She was like a spiritual magnet, attracting to the surface whatever was noble, whatever was right, whatever was pure, whatever was lovely, whatever was admirable. It was as if, in her presence, people became who they were created to be – at least for a moment. This is what I imagine Jesus is like. Alice revealed a glimpse of God.

Much love as always,
Rick & Cathy J

Hazel McD.

A beautiful friend of Charlotte's who helped us with the nights in hospital in Bath and Bristol, 2012.

Alice, my sweet, strong Alice.

She was the strongest warrior with the sweetest heart.

I was with Alice in the latter part of her life. My time with her began shortly before she became ill; a little while at home and through to the hospital. Although I spent most of my time with Alice tending to her every need when she was so ill, she would let me in, and would show me her shine like no other. Her fabulous personality would beam through, and she would give you the most precious, uplifting smile that we all knew and loved. She would never let her pain dampen her light.

I have a lot of very fond memories of Alice, even though my time with her occurred during some of her darkest days. It would often be just me and Alice in the hospital; we would watch some TV or read some of her favourite books, or play with some of her favourite 'twiddly' toys. Other times we would just be quiet and be together. In these moments are the memories that I hold most dear and close to my heart. In these moments of quiet Alice would be at her most calm and at peace. You could feel her trust in you, and her warmth radiated through her tiny body. She would snuggle in and somehow make you feel safe. I hope this was how she felt with me. These moments, when there were no seizures or pain, were the times when the most genuine and enlightening little girl would come free. You would be able to see her come into the room, and the whole room would come alive. However, these times didn't last long, but when they came, and I saw the true Alice, I would hold on tight to that moment.

This is when I realised that these moments had to be captured for Joanna and David. I started taking photographs of Alice, and although this was the part of her life that was the most awful to watch, I realised that this little girl didn't lose her faith or her smile, and this was what we needed to see. We needed to see this part of her life when her life was an uphill struggle, but this incredible little five-year-old saw the light in every day. This glimpse would be the highlight of my day, and I would be so excited to tell Joanna.

One day we ventured outside to the hospital garden. At this time Alice was often not able to walk or make it out of her room without a seizure, but on this day she was having a great day! She walked to the garden, with our help of course, and we had a glorious time in the sun. She felt all the flowers in the garden, and even took one inside to play with. This memory is held deep in my heart.

It was so hard to watch her little body go through so much pain at the young age of five. I have the utmost respect and gratitude for Joanna and David, who allowed me to spend time with their daughter. I spent most days and nights with Alice in Bath Royal United Hospital and Bristol Children's Hospital staying awake all night to log every seizure and to be with her when those awful, horrible seizures were happening. There were so many times I would just hold her tight to let her know it was OK, and it would be over soon. Joanna and I came up with a chart to log Alice's seizures as they were getting into such high figures in one day that we couldn't keep up! To watch this little body go through so much was just heartbreaking. I truly loved Alice from the bottom of my heart, and to this day caring for her has been one of the hardest things I have ever had to do, but by far the most rewarding. All my love goes to Joanna and David.

When my care for Alice started, I was going through a very hard patch of my life, but, through her guidance and love, Alice showed me how not to be afraid. She showed me gratitude, love, perseverance, faith, positivity and, most importantly, she showed me her light; the light of life. This little being was enduring so much and yet still had a smile on her bright, intelligent face. This lesson will always, always be with me. She showed me the light through my darkest days; I just hope I did the same for her. Her warmth is still with me and always will be. Her bright eyes and beaming smile. Her twiddly fingers and wiggly feet. She is missed, oh, so missed.

To my sweet, sweet Al. You are the star shining brighter than any other. Shine bright, sing loud and dance, my little one, dance!

Katie P.

Alice's cheerfully diligent ABA consultant in Bath, August 2010 to November 2011.

Dear Alice,

The moment I met you I saw a sparkle and a determination in your eyes. Your specific needs were different to anyone's I had ever worked with, but that didn't seem to matter to you as you had the strength to give everything your very best. You taught me so much, and you taught me that anything is possible.

We broke the strategies down and adapted them to you, and by your second team workshop, you were smiling when people used your personalised signs, and you had already started to use the signs all by yourself! You quickly saw the value of the skills we taught you, and utilised them in your fun and unique way. I can't imagine how difficult it must have been to not be able to say what you wanted to say, but hearing you try to fill in songs and even do your best to label your favourite Moo Cow (which we weren't even trying to teach you!) still warms my heart to this day.

You taught me that, no matter what life throws at you, you should never give up and always take the time to enjoy the wind in your face! I still see your beautiful smiling face every time I notice the wind. Thank you for teaching me how to truly enjoy the present moment.

Always in my heart,

Katie x

Rosie S.

One of Alice's talented tutors, September 2010 to September 2011.

Looking back on the time I worked with Alice, between September 2010 and September 2011, I now realise that she was truly at her best. Her personality shone when she was exploring her environment and joyfully interacting with everything she came into contact with. From wiggling her bottom watching *Boogie Beebies* to fiddling with flowers, bouncing on the trampoline, splashing and laughing in the bath, and stomping around the garden, Alice knew how to have a good time. I could never guess what she was going to be excited about from one moment to the next. As her walking and confidence improved, she allowed her feet to take her to whatever had grabbed her wandering attention.

Alice was a joy to be with, laughing and shrieking with delight at the smallest things – being thrown upside down on the sofa, twiddling a leaf between her finger and thumb, or seeing a banana being fetched at snack time. Part of the work that we did with Alice involved echoing every sound that she made in order to encourage her vocalisation. This meant we were all completely tuned in to Alice's language and way of communication, and it was a privilege to come a little closer into her world.

There are a few things that Alice and I did together that I'll never forget. Firstly, physical activities: swimming, trampolining, walking, running and rough-and-tumble play in the sitting room. Alice absolutely loved the intensity of these activities, and I felt humbled at participating in them with her. It was like all the difficulties that held her back so much of the time disappeared. In the pool, lying on her back and swirling around in the warm water, Alice's beautiful, content face was the picture of wonder. Her communication at these times was amazing: asking for more, shaking her arms up and down to get me to stand up and bounce with her again, looking up at me with her big, dancing brown eyes to find out what the next game would be. She pushed herself each day with gritty determination, revelling in her achievements and increasing independence.

Secondly, reading with Alice. Each afternoon and evening when I put her to bed, we would read together. Alice had clear favourites when it came to books, and I was her willing narrator. *A Squash and a Squeeze* was at the top of both our lists and I read it over and over, with Alice eagerly turning the pages, and anticipating the tickles that came with each 'squash and a squeeze'! The rhyme and the rhythm of her favourite stories sung to Alice in a mysterious way, and the delight she took in books is something I will always treasure.

And last, but by no means least, music. Music was in Alice's bones. It was a passion that filled her to the brim with elation, from the singing of birds in the morning, to her toilet song on the loo. In the world according to Alice, there was no event or activity that couldn't be enhanced with a song! Songs in the bath, car, garden, bed and kitchen; Mr Tumble's songs, and songs at BOP – it was as if everything became ten times more exciting when music was involved. I used to love watching Joanna sing lullabies to Alice before bed, and when no one was in the house, I would play the piano and sing for Alice, playing all my favourite songs for her. Now, when I sing the last verse of 'Bridge Over Troubled Water', I always think of Alice:

> Sail on, silver girl,
> Sail on by.
> Your time has come to shine.
> All your dreams are on their way;
> See how they shine, whoa.
> If you need a friend,
> I'm sailing right behind.
>
> Like a bridge over troubled water,
> I will ease your mind.
> Like a bridge over troubled water,
> I will ease your mind.
>
> *Bridge over Troubled Water*, Paul Simon

Alice taught me more than I could ever have imagined – patience, courage, creativity, a sense of humour, calmness; and when I walked where she walked and spoke to her in her shrieks and giggles, I learnt to take enjoyment in the small things, just like she did. For this, I will be eternally grateful.

Jenny I.

Jenny helped us cheerfully with Alice on the weekends in Bath for about six to nine months in 2010.

Alice

Alice with her deeply knowing, beautiful brown eyes.
Alice with her joyous smiles and oh-so-happy shrieks.
Alice in wonder at the images and characters on TV.
Alice twisting and twirling dangly toys between finger and thumb.
Alice snuggling up and snoozing on a lap, around 11am.
Alice reaching across the table and getting to her bowl first, relishing independence, loving her food.
Alice in the garden, with great purpose and independence, striding strongly round and about.
Alice on walks along the lane, stopping at the neighbour's flowery house sign, studying it up close.
Alice in her buggy, enjoying a sing-song along the way, twirling a daisy or buttercup between finger and thumb – what was that gorgeous twirling thing?
Alice, like an angel, settling down in bed with Moo, so completely happy, drifting off to rest awhile.
Alice, now at peace in a safe and loving haven beyond the rainbow…
Alice, as she was tested by the seizures. Something in her

expression told of her inner strength and acceptance as she rode the storm. So humbling…
Alice, a little angel on earth, now in her Heaven.
She came to teach us; she came to enrich our lives; she came to share her love…

Juliet J.

One of Alice's brilliant tutors, September 2010 to June 2012.

Lovely Alice.

It was such a privilege to know Alice, to work closely with her and see her enthusiasm, determination and tenacity. She had an enormous capacity for love and fun, and worked harder than anyone else I've known. I'm quite certain she taught me more than I taught her. Looking at books, exploring sensory items such as lights and textures, singing, chatting, Tacpac, doing physical exercises – she made every task a joy. It was wonderful to accompany her into BOP, her playgroup, and then Three Ways School. She took these changes to her routine in her stride, adapted quickly, and always became one of the most popular members of the class. Even when she was poorly in hospital, she made the best of her situation, and enjoyed exploring the outdoor play area, having a visit from the play therapist, or just chilling out together seeing what was on CBeebies.

My favourite memory of her: we'd taught her to ask to watch television by tapping her hand on her hip. One day, during a team meeting, we'd paused the television, and her therapists were chatting. She was clearly aggrieved that we weren't looking at her, and she advanced across the room towards me, a look of friendly, cheeky determination on her face, tapping her hip with increasingly larger movements.

If she had been verbal, she'd have been shouting, *Come on, Juliet, I'm talking to you here, listen to me!*

I feel so lucky to have known Alice and her wonderfully supportive family. I will treasure her memory forever. I picture her standing in her cot, Moo Cow at her side, with a huge smile on her face – the most wonderful start to a working day!

Anna M.

One of Alice's earnest tutors, September 2011 to June 2012.

Hi, Joanna,

Working with Alice and meeting her and her family changed me for the better. I didn't realise it at the time, but working with Alice was going to be one of the most valuable things I ever did.

When I first met Alice, I wasn't sure I could give her what she needed. I didn't feel like I was the best-placed person to support her. What I soon learnt, though, was that Alice didn't really need you to do much! Yes, she needed practical support in some ways, but she had such a happy and adventurous outlook that what she really seemed to enjoy the most was just having someone alongside her for the ride, to enjoy things with.

Alice taught me so much about myself and other people. She taught me that I am stronger than I had realised, and that I could love someone I hadn't known long as if they were my own family. Through Alice, I learnt about the kindness of others, most memorably the nurses who cared for her whilst she was in hospital. I am under no illusion: they did just as much caring for us (if not more) as they did for Alice. That was one of the many powerful things about Alice; she brought people together because she was such a joy to be around, and she led me to connect with people that I wouldn't have met otherwise.

One of the greatest things that you could get from Alice was a smile; you knew her smiles were always genuine, and her enjoyment was so contagious. Even when she wasn't well, she kept her spirit, always.

I am so thankful to Alice's family for sharing her with us; they were so generous with her time at a time when that was so difficult. I will forever be grateful for my time with Alice – it was only short, but it was one of the best gifts I have ever been given.

Naomi M.

Home help, holiday cover and my very dear friend, 2010 to 2013.

It's hard to know where to start as I write about Alice. I picture her sunny, kind, smiley face; her deep, warm brown eyes; her perfect eyebrows! Man, I was jealous of those eyebrows! And I can hear her little whoops of delight as she just went about her daily life with joy.

I remember some wonderful, happy times. On the beach in Cornwall always stands out. It was such a joy to watch her just soaking in her freedom with all of her senses: the wind in her hair, the sand under her feet (and occasionally in her mouth!), moving her arms and legs just as she pleased. I think that's why it's such a strong memory for me; on the vast beach, more than anywhere else, she was free to just be as she pleased.

I also loved to read stories to Alice, hoping, but never truly knowing, that she really loved them! We would joke about getting to Heaven and seeing Alice again and being told off: "You read that book to me *so* many times, and it was *so* boring!" Oh dear!

I remember the first time Alice signed. It was *so wonderful!* Of course, it was the sign to eat (Alice loved her food!), and it was a perfectly joyous moment! Seeing that she had made the connections and really learned something new – that, in turn, helped us to understand her a little better – was such an exciting prospect!

Part of me doesn't want to think about the latter part of Alice's life when her epilepsy began, and she had less and less energy and strength. But it is part of her journey, and there were such precious moments in that difficult time, too. At first, she began fitting when she started to drift off to sleep, and it was heart-wrenching to watch her desperately trying to stay awake to avoid the episodes. But what strength and determination! She was a little fighter!

As I remember it, when Alice started taking the epilepsy medication it would work for a while, but then as her body got used to it her fits would get worse again and the doses had to be gradually increased and increased again. It was horrible to watch the epilepsy beat the medication like that. I'll never forget that medication: Epilim. It was bright purple, it almost looked like blackberry syrup, and on one occasion Joanna and I (I'll share the blame) spilt half the bottle on the pristine cream carpet of a Cornish holiday cottage! Oops!

The time I spent with Alice in hospital was really hard because it was the real beginning of the end, and it did feel as though she had begun to slip away because she just didn't have the energy she had once had. But it was *the most* tremendous privilege to be there with her in those precious moments, cuddling her, stroking her hair, holding her soft little hand and just loving her.

Thank you so much, Joanna and David, for giving me that incredible time with her. Those moments in hospital, alongside the Cornish beach days, I will cherish and treasure until Alice and I meet again.

Charlotte J.

Home help and wonderful nanny, March 2010 to November 2013.

Spending time with Alice was like therapy. Like the best therapy money could buy… only it was free. It didn't matter what was going on in my own life; when I walked into the living room, where she would be bopping up and down in front of the TV, or her bedroom after she'd had her nap, and she gave me her usual beaming smile, all my personal problems seemed to just dissolve, and I could only really feel warmth and love around her.

Most of my memories of Alice are from before she began to struggle. I don't know whether that's because there were a lot more happier memories or whether my mind has blanked out some of the tougher ones. But I do know that, even during the hardest times, she still clung on to her pure and innocent appreciation of life, finding joy in the simplest of things. It's as if she saw and appreciated all the beautiful, small things around us, that most people would miss.

No one will ever quite compare to Alice. She was a true shining star, and I will forever cherish every moment I shared with her and every memory I hold of her.

Amanda M.

Home help and our cheerful nanny, March 2007 to November 2008.

When I came to your home in Rutland, one day after work to meet you, I was nervous. I had never been a nanny! You welcomed me with a big smile, and I saw this gorgeous baby over your shoulder. Just six months old! Big, dark eyes, and a smile that could melt your heart!

You offered me the job, and from that moment my world changed.

Alice was a happy baby. Smiley and very relaxed. The weaning journey was fun and messy. ☺ Exploring the garden was incredible too.

Six months passed, and when Alice got to a year, I remember you asking me a question. "Do you think she should be doing more?" It wasn't something I had thought about! She was a fab eater and sleeper, and happy. What more could you want?

The next few weeks and months were happy and sad at times. Doctors' appointments, and lots of research. I remember global developmental delay being mentioned, and trips to Africa and America being spoken about. All I could do at this time was offer support and love. Plenty of love.

Soon enough, there were therapists and helpers, and Alice showed us how strong she was. I helped her learn to sit and kneel and crawl and stand. It was magical, yet sad. I have memories of Burghley House, Legoland and the London Eye. The cuddles, the love.

Through this time, I saw strength in the Whittakers and became a Christian, and still use my study Bible today. Daily I sang 'My Jesus, My Saviour' whilst holding Alice and being with the family and their gorgeous boys.

My time with Alice and her family was the most rewarding time of my life. I learnt so much in a short space of time. I feel very blessed to have been a part of Alice's short but fulfilled life.

Sorry this is so long, Joanna. When I began to think about my time with you all, I kept thinking about it all. I know I was young, but you all taught me so, so much. My memories are all such happy ones.

I want to thank you for having me in your life.

Lots of love to all of you.

xxxx

Liz W.

Our faithful nanny and earnest carer for Alice, November 2008 to November 2009.

Alice loved music, singing and touch. She was very sensory, and the pleasure she would get from sitting on a pony, smelling a flower, or splatting in paint was infectious. She may have been slower to develop than some children but watching her learn to walk and communicate was so rewarding. She liked routine, and she liked people, and when you connect with someone who is 'different' you too will find a bucket of happiness fills and overflows.

Before Alice, I hadn't worked with children with additional needs, and while I wasn't worried, I didn't expect it to be as rewarding as it was. I fell in love with Alice and how she communicated and shone joy in her own way. I have gone on to care for children with many similar needs and conditions all thanks to Alice and her family.

Love Liz x

Janet J.

Housekeeper and friend, September 2006 to November 2009.

I have thought long and hard about writing about Alice and have found it very difficult to get something down on paper.

It's so hard as my memories of Alice are very personal and dear to me. Somehow writing them down changes the intimacy I experienced from the day she arrived.

Sadness when it was revealed that her life would be very different to the boys. The tears in our eyes as you sat on the grass under that huge beautiful tree. The tree that Alice would look up into as she sat on the swing. Her eyes full of wonderment as she watched the leaves flutter in the wind. Her interaction with the boys. The joy of getting into Scally's bed. I feel inadequate expressing in words how that little touch of star dust changed all of our lives.

Love you, Janet.

Sarah H-B.

Alice's perfect paediatric physiotherapist in Rutland, September 2008 to April 2009.

Alice... well, what can I say that hasn't been said by all who met her? There are many children whom I have the pleasure to meet and treat and call my little friends, but Alice is one I still often think about, and she brings a smile to my face.

Her smile and her enduring patience with me were amazing; she always seemed to enjoy her sessions and cope with my endless singing! Her smile and look were precious and will remain with me. Her family will also remain with me, and I will always remember the way her brothers would look at Alice with deep love when joining some sessions. Joanna's love is endless, and yes, it was very difficult for her to see her child doing exercises, but without the love and support from Joanna and the rest of the family, Alice would not have achieved the strides she made.

Alice will always live in our hearts and thoughts, and I feel privileged to have known her and her family.

Jane W.

Alice's dynamic paediatric occupational therapist in Rutland, September 2008 to November 2009.

A Thank-You to Alice

I was very privileged, some years ago, to meet a wonderful family who had a little girl who amazed, challenged, stimulated and developed me as a therapist.

Her name was Alice.

Alice made me think again about the world of sensory processing, and how I needed to adapt and grow my clinical practice in order to meet her unique needs.

Thank you, Alice, for making me a better therapist.

Thank you, Alice, for all the fun we had.

Thank you, Alice, for all the guts and determination you showed throughout all our therapy sessions.

Thank you, Alice, for being willing to engage with all the mad, active, sensory-based play with 'bells and whistles' on that we undertook together. I too felt like falling into a happy, exhausted sleep after our therapy sessions!

Thank you, Alice, for introducing me to your wonderful family, especially your amazing mum.

Special memories of a special little girl.

Jane x

Caroline H.

Alice's kind speech and language therapist, August 2008 to December 2009.

Alice and her family were a delight to work with. When I first met Alice, the thing that struck me about her was what a happy little girl she was. Her brothers doted on her and were very eager to join in with our sessions to help Alice. She already had an amazing support network of family and therapists, and I was unsure at first what I could add. I learnt a lot as a therapist from Alice, and enjoyed the fun we had in joint SPOT (joint speech and occupational therapy) sessions. Her family were brilliant at reading Alice's non-verbal cues. Anything I suggested we try, Joanna and the family were willing to practise at home.

Working with Alice was a joy, and I certainly felt like a member of the family. One particular memory I have of Alice was when I was travelling back from work one day. I saw the boys at the side of the road with their nanny (her car had broken down). I stopped and offered them a lift, ringing Joanna to ask if this was OK. The whole family later popped round to my house with a delightful home-made snowdome which I still have this day. Alice looked so happy that day as the boys handed me their gift. When Alice smiled, we all melted.

I feel very honoured to have been a part of her life

and to have known her and her whole family. Alice taught me so much, and I truly believe I became a better person having met her and her family. Thank you all.

Caroline x

Notes

Extract on p. 15 from 'Memory' (Elaine Page). Written by Andrew Lloyd Webber, Tim Rice and T. S. Eliot © Copyright Faber and Faber Ltd

Extract on p. 57 from Little Fires Everywhere by Celeste Ng (Little, Brown, 2017). Reproduced with permission from Little, Brown Book Group Ltd.

Extract on p. 144 from Behind the Scenes at the Museum by Kate Atkinson, published by Transworld. Reproduced by permission of The Random House Group Ltd. ©1994

Extract on p. 235 from 'I Can Only Imagine' by Bart Millard and MercyMe © Copyright 2002 Simpleville Music (adm Small Stone Media BV/Song Solutions www.songsolutions.org). All rights reserved. Used by permission.

Extract on p. 267 from 'Bridge Over Troubled Water'. Words & Music by Paul Simon © Copyright 1969 Paul Simon Music. All Rights Administered by Songs of Universal, Inc. All Rights Reserved. International Copyright Secured. Used by permission of Hal Leonard Europe Limited.